MW01679172

STRESS LESS IN 90 DAYS

YOUR GUIDE TO BEAT BURNOUT, BUILD RESILIENCE AND ACTUALLY ENJOY YOUR DAILY LIFE

VICTORIA SMITH

GIRL TRIES LIFE MEDIA

Book design by Sheena Lidgett

ISBN 978-0-9950055-1-8 (paperback)
ISBN 978-0-9950055-3-2 (ebook)
ISBN 978-0-9950055-2-5 (audiobook)

stresslessin90days.ca

TESTIMONIALS

"*Stress Less in 90 Days* was a wonderful gift I gave myself and I would 100% recommend this 12 week program to anyone who is not quite satisfied with how they are managing their current stress levels."
Jen S., Calgary, Canada

"*Stress Less in 90 Days* provided me with the framework to organize my thoughts, to move forward positively and not be intimidated by seeming obstacles which could be turned into positive steps."
Lynn R, Scotland

"I feel better equipped to deal with life because of this course's tools and its journal reflections, which have ultimately encouraged me to treat myself better."
Wendy W., Calgary, Canada

"The Stress Less in 90 Days program gave me the tools to work on my stress without being stressful!."
Sarah M, Canada

"[Stress Less in 90 Days] gave me so many tools that I can use to better myself personally, at work, and in relationships with friends and family. I highly recommend Victoria's coaching for anyone looking for it."
Nicole S., Canada

"[We] have brought Victoria in to speak on stress management on two occasions. Both times, Victoria did a fantastic job of presenting the material in a highly engaging, interesting and thoughtful manner. Attendee feedback was incredibly positive. We'd work with Victoria again in a heartbeat!"
Mount Royal University, Alumni Department

"Victoria has energy that is absolutely unmatched and she is deeply invested in the wellbeing of her clients and peers. She is an asset to any speaker roster and throughout her sessions you will reflect, learn and even laugh out loud! I would not hesitate to recommend Victoria to anyone."

ATB Entrepreneur Centre

To my fellow stress balls. We've got this.

RASH DECISIONS

It started with a rash on my ass.

I was on a weekend getaway with my mom, a much-needed break, in Victoria, Canada. I had been working sixty-hour weeks with my husband living over six thousand kilometers away in Scotland, chatting via Skype at the oddest of hours, and living alone was feeling pretty...lonely.

Hence the trip. It was our second day and while changing my clothes to get ready for our first adventure, I noticed a patch of red, flaky skin on my left butt cheek. It was itchy. Having grown up with eczema, I am no stranger to the odd skin issue. I put it down to the hotel's detergent, but as the day went on the itching got worse, driving me wild. It didn't stop. Forty-eight hours later, away from adventure and back in Calgary, back at work, the rash had spread down my left leg and up the side of my back. It hurt. A lot. It felt like little bolts of lightning shooting up my body at random intervals.

I went to the doctor. Under bright, fluorescent lighting, I unbuckled my pants, my cheeks flushed with embarrassment. My doctor took a brief glance then proceeded to spend a good five minutes asking me about how I was feeling stress-wise. How many hours was I working? Was I unhappy? What was my mental state like? Did I feel motivated in any area of my life? Did my heart ever race? Had I ever had a panic attack?

The diagnosis was shingles, a viral infection that causes a painful rash. Same family as chickenpox, except traditionally you don't see people getting shingles until their fifties or sixties. Traditionally.

"No offence," I said to my doctor, "but I don't exactly look like the advert for shingles." I remembered my sixty-year old father getting a shingles vaccine the previous year.

My doctor nodded. "You're right, but I'm seeing more and more young people getting shingles due to stress." He went on to explain that stress didn't directly cause shingles, but chronic stress does a great job of battering the immune system, allowing the doors to illness to be flung wide open.

I was embarrassed. I was twenty-seven and shouldn't be overwhelmed by a full-time job and a long-distance relationship. Plenty of my friends seemed to be killing it at work and at home. Why couldn't I?

I certainly didn't enjoy telling my employer that I had shingles, a virus more common in the elderly. So, while I couldn't be physically at work as the virus is contagious, I fired up my laptop and worked from home five or six hours a day. I was physically exhausted, drained, and not getting good sleep. The agonizing rash and jolts of nerve pain that ran the length of my body made it hurt to sit or lay down, walking was pure misery. I'd get myself into the oddest of positions, balance my laptop precariously on a pillow on my lap, cushions underneath my butt and work away as though I wasn't seriously ill. I pushed through. Two weeks of this agony and as soon as I could be back at the office, I was.

Time moved on. My husband moved to Canada and certain stressors were removed, but work continued carrying on with a heavy load. I'd wake early to get to work before anyone else, fueled by massive amounts of Starbucks, and ride the waves of anxiety and stress that came with a job where I couldn't control many of the outcomes. Half my job was as a corporate event planner. It's the kind of job where you can have the most detailed Excel spreadsheet and plan an event to total precision only to have the caterer show up late. Or maybe there's a leak at the venue. Or the bus for guests showed up without seatbelts, and your company policy will not allow you to use a bus without seatbelts, and now twenty executives are sweating in their suits waiting for multiple taxis to arrive. No stress there. No, sir.

Then I became pregnant with my son. The juggling began. My parents announced they were getting divorced after more than thirty years - add a new ball. I found out my Dad had cheated on my mom and I ended up being the one to tell her - add another one. Oh, and to top it all off, a global recession was underway, the price of oil crashed and there were definitely going to be layoffs at work. Another ball and another and another. Until…

The balls dropped.

That familiar rash on my ass returned. I called the maternity clinic and they sent me to the hospital. This time I hoped I'd caught it early enough to get a vaccine to minimize the pain. I was six months pregnant, so just like any other person that far along in pregnancy, they send you to the maternity ward where you get assessed whether you have a broken arm, contractions, or, as in my case, shingles. Eyes widened when I said I suspected a return of the virus. They shuffled me off to the furthest room from all the other glowing mamas to be. Doctors and nurses donned yellow gowns and blue latex gloves before entering the room and assessing me. I felt like a buzzing neon caution sign. Again, I felt like a failure, like I couldn't handle the stress of normal people, but this time it doubly stung because my health was now impacting my unborn child. What kind of mother would I be if I couldn't even offer my child the carefree waterbed of its dreams? Mom-guilt starts early.

Those few months were some of my worst. It was all just too damn much. My support systems dried up. My mom was going through her own trauma with the divorce. I didn't want to be around my Dad. My husband did his best, but was equally overwhelmed by all the things. My brother was a great listener, but I didn't want to burden him with more than necessary as he had his own new baby at home.

And then, after what felt like an eternity of pregnancy, my son was born. I pushed for two hours with a failed epidural (oh yeah, they don't tell you that can happen) and then he was born. I loved him instantly, and yet, only an hour after my husband and my mom left the hospital for some much-needed sleep, I was sobbing to the nurse about how I couldn't do it, I didn't want to let my kid down. The nurse saw the total panic in my eyes, took my son to the nursery so I could get some sleep, and I lay there thinking about all the ways I was going to screw this up.

I had very few friends with kids, so I felt isolated in motherhood. My son would cry for hours on end, colic causing his insides to writhe in pain and his lungs to scream in agony. And then postpartum depression hit, dropping me off an emotional cliff and leaving me for the buzzards to pick at.

One random afternoon of yet more screaming (my son) and silent tears (mine), I picked up the phone and dialed a local charity called Families Matter. Among many services, they support women with postpartum depression. My intake call was forty-seven minutes long and I sobbed my eyes out to the counsellor about all the things, my child included, that were choking me. She listened. She told me it would be okay. She said it was natural to feel this way. She told me I wasn't alone. And she booked me in for my first session with my designated counsellor.

I'd been to counselling before, but this was different. This changed my life. Little by little, I felt more in control. Session by session, I built my toolkit of strategies to handle hard moments. We didn't only talk about my son and motherhood. We discussed the pain of my parents' divorce. We talked about how unhappy I was at work. We talked about how challenging change is and why it's hard for most people to tackle one life change, let alone three or four simultaneously. She held space for me, encouraged me, and helped me to rebuild my life.

After our final session together, I continued this work on my own. All I wanted to do was help others, even a little bit as much as my counsellor had helped me. While I love the experience of counselling, I didn't feel called to it in the same way as coaching.

Counselling is incredible to help you process what you've been through and how it's affecting you. Coaching can help you move forward and achieve whatever that new desired state is. What I love about coaching is that it's action-oriented. You can use counselling and coaching in tandem, or you can do them sequentially, but they serve different purposes.

I share these stories with you from the get-go so that you have a sense of who I am and why I wrote this book. I am not a psychologist or a doctor. I am a coach who has helped many women to make a path off the stress treadmill and towards a stress-less future.

I want to make it clear that I am coming at this book, and frankly at my life, from a state of privilege. I am a university-educated, white, cisgender woman. I don't know what it is to experience racism or bigotry firsthand. These naturally add an extra layer of stress onto an individual. While I can't know what it is to walk through that stress, I do know that the strategies I learned and will share in this book are high-level enough that it shouldn't matter what combination of stressors you're experiencing. Even though these strategies should work, I don't have the lived experience of disability, racism, etc. There are systemic changes that need to be made to lessen these stressors.

I launched my business, Stress Less Ladies, to help women significantly reduce their stress, so that they can actually enjoy their daily lives instead of feeling guilty they were supposed to be doing something else. I do this through coaching (one-to-one or group), online courses and corporate workshops.

One day I was giving a workshop at a glossy tech company in town. It was my biggest speaking gig to date, and I had great engagement from the audience and questions about their stress management. As I was wrapping up and chatting to a friend that worked at the company, I was introduced to a woman with bouncy red hair, tired eyes and a big smile. Her name was Jen, and she'd been far too busy (stressed!) to attend the workshop. I told Jen about my job and how I help women to reduce their stress. She smiled, as most people I talk to do, and told me how she could definitely use some stress relief. The difference is that most people I talk with say they want to reduce stress, and then they do absolutely nothing about it. They don't know how. They get busy. They feel they have no time.

A busy mom of two, a lawyer and a hugely competent person, Jen believed that stress was just par for the course. "I'm kind of wired this way, I always have been," she said in our first session. I smiled and nodded, in the back of my head thinking we'll see. I could tell she was super skeptical.

Skeptics are my favorite.

Meet Jen

Jen was ready to be less stressed. She had a lot on her plate. A senior lawyer, her work had a major impact at the company that she worked at. It also had a lot of visibility. When things went well, people saw it, and when they didn't, they saw that too. Jen was (and is) a high achiever. She wanted to do a great job, but she was struggling with the sustainability of long hours, two young kids, and the intensity of her workload. Her health took a toll. She'd get epic migraines. And she'd even done all the things that had been suggested to her. She'd done counselling, she got massages when her body got too tight, she went for the mother of all walks, and it still didn't make much of a difference.

So, Jen decided to go all-in with me and commit to the 90-day program. She took action, because she was well aware that if something didn't change, her stress would spiral out of control. She showed up. Not just for me, but for herself.

Who is this book for?

Like Jen, if you're sick of constantly being stressed or reliving the same stressors again and again, this book is for you. You might have tried a number of band-aid self-care solutions but that bubble bath alone isn't cutting it! You go to bed early but you're not sleeping. You dream of what it would be like to not work through lunch and have your inbox in a constant state of overflow.

You are ready to show up. Consistently. You're in it to feel better. Not for anyone else. For you.

Let me repeat that – this is about feeling better for *you*. Of course, this will have a knock-on effect for your family, friends or coworkers. When we feel differently, we show up differently. But you have to want this for you. When clients come to me wanting change to help their families… that's tied to guilt. You're pushing yourself towards the end goal as opposed to being pulled to it by a desire for change.

If you are in the midst of trauma, I urge you to seek professional help first. This book is not meant to help you walk through the throes of grief, trauma or mental illness. I always recommend counselling and I don't know a single person that couldn't benefit from therapy. The strategies in this book won't add to your trauma, but they aren't enough to fully process a recent divorce, the loss of a loved one, being laid off from your dream job, or an assault. Remember, counselling is to process what has happened, and then coaching can help you move forward. While counselling and *Stress Less in 90 Days* can be done in tandem, and I have clients that choose to go that route frequently, this program is not a substitute for experiences that require professional psychological support.

Jen quickly realized that these weren't your average stress-less tips. Over twelve weeks I guided her through key foundations into lasting stress reduction. We talked through her challenges from the previous week, then set action items she'd work on in the week ahead. Almost every week Jen would have some journal questions to reflect on as homework. She found that the journal questions were often where the learning cemented itself and more a-ha moments would arise.

Some weeks were better than others. Some weeks, her workload was a dumpster fire, other weeks she was rocking consistent self-care. At one point, she wondered if the only solution was to quit her job, even though she loved the people and the organization's mission. So many people who are stressed at work think that their only solution is to quit. But Jen persevered, showed up each week and did the work — the internal work.

I won't lie - there was another little bump in the road during our coaching - about four weeks in, Jen got shingles. We laughed, because isn't it ironic that someone who is trying to stress less would get shingles? But that's what the body is good at. As soon as you get off the wild, frantic train, your body takes a sigh of relief and lets everything out. In this case, it let out shingles.

But still, Jen showed up.

How do I use this book?

Stress Less in 90 Days is specifically designed to be your path to managing your stress over three months. We intentionally do NOT throw you in at the deep end for you to fail. Sink or swim? Not here. Here we believe in giving you the foundations to smash your goal to stress less. Each week, you will have specific strategies to try that will build up over the weeks. Think of it like getting a new tool for your stress less toolbox each week. There's a reason we don't focus on self-sabotage until week five. Can you imagine if on week one, day one I was like "BAM! We're going to dive into why the heck you quit on yourself"? That would be intense, right? So no, we're not going to do that.

Whether you choose to read the book through once and then go back week by week, or only read one week at a time, that's up to you. Neither one is better than the other. What I urge, however, is that you *do the work*. Each week, which is a complete chapter, ends with a recap of self-reflection questions for you to journal, and some exercises for you to try.

In addition to this book you'll be able to download a digital companion workbook. We've all bought personal development books, thought to ourselves *Huh, that was interesting* and then never actually applied the strategies. We read the book but didn't do the work. Promise me, you'll show up for yourself and do the exercises. My clients attest that they make one heck of a difference.

So, right now, set aside two hours a week for this work. That two hours includes time to read the chapter as well as time to do the exercises. Just imagine I was coaching you – you'd set aside the time for our calls, right? Set aside time for yourself.

There is a daily element to this work. Change doesn't only happen in your scheduled two-hour window. It happens when you're shopping for groceries, or decide to experiment by swapping out a coping mechanism that doesn't serve you. The focused work is roughly two hours a week, but the engrained learning will show up when least expected.

It sounds simple, but simple doesn't mean easy. Don't expect it to always be easy. This program is laid out for you, one step at a time. If you set aside time and do the work, it's simple, but we all know that showing up for yourself can be the hardest part. You will have bumps in the road. I've had clients start working with me while going through some of the most difficult things you can go through. A rough trimester of pregnancy, a parent in the hospital, or a partner asking for a divorce. Remember Jen? She got shingles! Hell, I got shingles.

Life isn't going to throw you the perfect three months to do this. What matters is that you keep coming back to it, *especially* if it's a hard week. You need it all the more during those times.

Find Someone to Be Accountable To

Part of what made this program so different for Jen was that she was checking in with someone weekly. And not just a "Hey I went to spin class," text to a friend, but a real check in on what worked over the past week, what didn't, and what she'd change going forward. She was finally accountable to someone other than herself.

Something magic happens when you know that you'll be connecting with someone to update them on your progress. You show up differently.

Studies show that we are up to 95% more likely to achieve the change we're after when we're accountable to someone. I always say "Up to 95%" is a huge range. That could be 5%, 55%, or the full 95%. That's because you and I both know it matters *who* you are accountable to.

In university, I made a commitment with a friend in my dorm to go to the gym three times a week. We were going to wake up at 6 a.m., support one another, kick each other's butts. Know how many times we went? Twice. That's because we weren't the right people to hold one another accountable. We were both a little too scared. We gave up on ourselves all the time, so naturally when one person said they didn't or couldn't go that day, the other phoned it in as well.

Find that person that will check in with you weekly. Who is your tough love person that holds you to the highest version of yourself? If you don't feel you have a person like this in your life right now, that's okay. It can be a doctor, a coach like myself, a family member, or a colleague. Or you can find someone that wants to do this program with you. Get on board together. Make it your little reading/accountability/stress-less club. However you can make it happen, make sure there is someone in your corner. You can always drop me a DM @stresslessladies and let me know how you're doing with the program. I'd love to hear from you. It doesn't mean that I can be your accountability person, but sometimes just the act of sharing that you're doing something is enough to kick start that accountability and motivation.

It's two years later and you know what? Jen is thriving, and during a global pandemic! She's thriving so much that she's taken on a crazy cool promotion, enjoys being at work (she didn't quit the job!) and is navigating the changes that life throws her way. Do things get stressful? Of course they do, but she consistently practices the strategies she and I spent twelve weeks building, and that makes all the difference. She showed up and she still shows up for herself.

I can't promise you perfect. I can promise you that this won't be perfect. But if you continue to show up for the next twelve weeks, I promise you'll see a difference.

Don't believe me? Let's hear what Jen has to say.

A Note from Jen

Since I completed the 12-week program with Victoria, I had to take a bit of time to really reflect on the impact this work has had on how I think about stress generally, my strategies for managing that stress and my levels of happiness overall. Coming in, I was rather resigned to my daily experience with stress and felt like because I had chosen a career where stress and pressure are the norm, the impacts I was experiencing with my health (e.g. physical pain from tension, chronic headaches and migraines), my relationships (e.g. not being present at home with my two young children and husband when I wasn't working) and my work (e.g. feeling reactive and emotional instead of calm and composed) were something I just had to cope with.

"Not so!" said Victoria and she was right – Victoria is the kind of person you want in your mom-tribe: she cares, is smart, pragmatic and solutions-oriented and has a robust, research-based program with tons of good information. Now that I am through the program, the stress is still there (and will always be), but I have good, practical strategies in place for making sure that it doesn't totally dominate my life. I have fewer migraines, am able to be more present when I am at home with my family and don't find that the stress of my work influences how I operate quite so much. I'm just generally in a better place and know that I have good tools to fall back on when the pressure kicks up. Working with Victoria was such a wonderful gift that I gave myself and I would 100% recommend *Stress Less in 90 Days* to anyone who is not quite satisfied with how they are managing their current stress levels.

Not all my clients are like Jen. Most are, but not all. The most important key to Jen's success was that she showed up and kept at it. If you can do that, you will see change.

I want to recognize you for accepting that things need to change and taking the action to start. That in and of itself shows you're brave and courageous. While it can be easier to stay stuck, it is a brave person who reaches out for the tools to make their life better. You don't have to feel brave to be brave. Simply show up.

You've got this. I know it.

WEEK ZERO

CHIC PRINCIPLES OF PREPARATION

WHETHER YOU'VE SEEN THE MOVIE *ROCKY* OR NOT, I BET YOU KNOW the training montage. Buh-buh-bahhhhhh, buh-buh-bahhhhhh. Okay, I'm not gonna sing, but you know what I'm talking about. Rocky is a small-time boxer with a goal of fighting the heavy-weight champion, so he trains for the fight of his life. He runs through the streets of Philly, someone tosses him an apple, he pummels an animal carcass and shows us his ability to do one-armed push-ups. The music rises and Rocky is finally ready. He ascends the stairs of the Philadelphia Museum of Art and raises his arms in the air. The music peaks. He's done it, he's ready!

It feels so good to see.

Here's the thing – that training montage is two minutes and forty-one seconds long. It is the ultimate highlight reel. Last time you worked on a major goal, did you get a training montage? Did you get a *Rocky* moment? Even this morning as I worked on my own fitness goal, a lot of it was sweating, beet-red in the face and schlepping up the mini-mountain next to my home. It felt good afterwards, but it wasn't a two minutes and forty-one seconds inspirational *Rocky* moment.

I think we'd all love it if life worked that way, but it doesn't. Our desire for instant gratification often has us giving up before we've even begun. I looked up how long a traditional boxing training camp takes – twelve weeks. Ding ding ding! Time put in and consistency is what matters. Isn't it lucky that you're about to go through your own twelve-week stress less training camp?

This particular training camp is built around four principles:

Core needs
Honesty
Incremental gains
Consistency.

CHIC. Easy to spell and remember but what does it mean?

We love the montage. It's exciting and action packed. But that two minutes is months in the making. It's hard work and effort that often goes unnoticed. When you're in it, when you're doing the work, it can be easy to get discouraged because results don't happen immediately. They build over time. You have to be prepared for the long haul to see lasting change. The CHIC principles will help you prepare.

Why is it important to prepare? Quite simply, you get better outcomes when you are prepared. Would you go into a job interview without prepping for certain questions or how you'll talk about your work experience? Unlikely. Would you show up for your big exam without studying or getting a good night's sleep? Not if you want good grades! If you had to fire an employee, would you just say "See ya later!" or would you take some time to thoughtfully explain why this person is no longer a fit for your organization and treat them like a human being? The latter, I'm sure.

Preparation leads to better results – period. So, let's take this pre-week, Week Zero, to get yourself prepared mentally and physically, putting you in much better shape to achieve your goals.

Principle # 1: Core Needs

Have you ever been irrationally stressed and you can't quite put a finger on it? Everything on the surface is fine, but you're vibrating with stress and anxiety? Something is off. It's making you angry, frustrated or fidgety. If only you could put your finger on it.

Often when there's no situational stressor that we can point to, the answer lies in our basic needs not being met. When you feel this way it's important to check in with your basic physical needs: sleep, nutrition and movement. When one or more of these three are out of sync, you're going to feel crummy or low in energy which adds to your stress. I don't expect you to become a super sleeper, master nutritionist or awesome athlete in one week, but I do want to raise your awareness of which of these core needs could use a little TLC in the next seven days and beyond.

Let's start with sleep.

Your Guide to Get More Zzz's

If you are not sleeping well, you're probably stressed. As a mother of two small children, I had no idea how pivotal sleep would be to my mood, my energy and my outlook on life until a solid night's sleep was taken from me. My kids are five and three. It's very rare that I sleep for a consistent amount of time before someone will wake up screaming from a nightmare. Or maybe it's an accident. Or they'll just wake up early, full of beans. Or they're tired and want tucked in again. Or hey, what about the cat? The cat starts crying because he's lonely.

When you sleep well, you think more clearly. You can solve problems. You're less irritable and less likely to get upset over minor inconveniences. I used to work in a coffee shop and I have legitimately seen grown adults lose their shit when we had run out of their chosen milk because the delivery was late. Let's not be the gal who sweats the small stuff – almond milk is not life or death.

If you're not sleeping well, you're more prone to forgetfulness. So, whether you're trying to remember that tomorrow is pajama day at daycare or you need to remember tiny details for a client meeting, our memory is critical to helping us function in an optimal state. Forget a lot of things and you're likely to be more stressed because your kid is the odd one out with no pajamas or you lose the client because of a flub.

Ever seen the Pixar movie *Inside Out*? The characters Joy and Sadness are trying to find their way through Riley's brain back to headquarters. Riley falls asleep, and that's when they come across two workers who are examining memories and getting rid of the ones she no longer needs. "Four years of piano! Yeah, these look pretty faded. Save Chopsticks and Heart and Soul. Get rid of the rest," says one of the workers. The other worker sucks the memories into a machine and deletes them. I don't know about you, but that sounds pretty much like my memory of piano lessons. Sleep allows your brain to do this hard work of dissecting what stays and what goes, so you don't have to hold it all in.

But for many, solid sleep eludes us. Do you struggle to sleep through the night? You go to bed at a set time with the best of intentions, yet wake through the night worrying about whatever is going on in your life. You're stressed, so you sleep poorly, but to reduce the stress you know you need to sleep better. It's a bit of a chicken or the egg situation.

So, which do you deal with first – the sleep or the stress? This week, we'll deal with the actions you can take to get a better sleep. We have the rest of the program to focus on stress management, but this week it's about paving the way to make the whole process easier.

I'm not going to beat you over the head with a whole chapter on sleep – I almost did (it's that important) then I trimmed it down to the below experiments for you to test. You may have tried one or more of these before, so again the goal isn't to be perfect in all areas, but to pick the juiciest one to try and experiment with its impact on your rest.

- **Minimize stimulants an hour before bed.** These include: blue light (phones, computers, TV, etc.), caffeine, alcohol, snacks. I know, I know I also love a G&T with some chips while watching a show, but in that last hour before bed minimize activities and inputs that are going to amp up your system rather than help wind it down. Try slow-down activities like reading a physical book, a shower, light stretching, or cuddling with your pet (or loved one).

- **Keep the phone out of your bedroom.** If you want to reduce the temptation of this tech stimulant, get a physical alarm clock. You can even buy one that wakes you up by gradually increasing the light as opposed to that oppressive "beep, beep, beep" that jolts you awake. A much more pleasant way to start the day.
- **Increase your sleep drive – don't nap late!** Your sleep drive is your body's need for sleep. You know when your head is READY to hit the pillow? That's sleep drive. To make sure you have enough of it at bedtime, minimize naps throughout the day and the length of naps 5-6 hours before your bedtime.
- **Create a bedtime routine**. Children thrive off routines. Routines cue their bodies and mind that sleep is coming when they do the same set of activities at the same time before they sleep. We are giant children. Or big babies. Whatever you prefer. Baby or child, giant or not, build a routine to put yourself to bed like a baby.
- **Keep the same bedtime and wake up time.** If you're prone to going to bed later and sleeping in on the weekends, your body feels the impact Monday morning, similar to jet lag. It's not just the Monday blues. It's because for two days you trained your body to shift its sleep pattern. As boring as it sounds, if you can go to bed at the same time and wake up at the same time, your body will thank you for it.

GIANT CAVEAT – know your season of life. If you have a newborn at home, disregard any and all tips on sleep here. You do you and focus on surviving this new phase of life.

For everyone else, pick one and give it a go this week. See if that helps improve your sleep, and if not, move on to the next. This is all about experimentation.

Nutrition

When I did my training as a health and a life coach, I remember there was a video breaking down over one hundred diets in the space of ten minutes. I thought no, surely that wasn't possible. But what it comes down to is that every diet out there manipulates the percentage of carbs to protein to fat. And it's true. If you break down any diet, the fundamental principle is based on the proportion of each of those categories.

Now, I wholeheartedly disagree with diets. From intermittent fasting to macros, from Weight Watchers to juicing, the only methodology that I endorse when it comes to the foods that you put in your mouth is Intuitive Eating.

Here's why – 95% of diets fail. Statistically, diets do not work in the long run. Any of us can do anything for a short period of time. We can restrict, we can buy the programs, get meal kits to our doors, but it's much harder to make a diet a lifestyle. Why? Because we don't want to feel restricted. It's in our DNA to feast and avoid famine, and diets are an artificial form of famine.

And then there's the stress – diets are stressful, plain and simple. Diets make us feel less than or too big, like we're a failure, like we are defined by the numbers on the scale or the label of our clothes. You are more than that goddamn number and you need to know it.

I read a personal development book once where the author said something along the lines of would you respect a woman who can't respect herself because she quits every diet she starts? No. Every single human being deserves respect regardless of whether they've been able to stick to a diet or not. End of discussion.

What I want for you is for you to feel energetic and vibrant. Get rid of the numbers. No more obsession with counting calories, weighing food, measuring your meals on some sort of a point system. No more punishing yourself with activity in order to "earn" that dessert. That's bullshit.

Enter Intuitive Eating.

What is Intuitive Eating? *Intuitive Eating*, developed by Elyse Resch and Evelyn Tribole, focuses on how to nurture your body, find your equilibrium, learn to listen to your needs and provide your body with gentle nutrition.

Young children, babies in particular, are the perfect example of intuitive eaters. They eat when they're hungry, they stop when they're full. I remember feeding my babies and whether there was still milk in the bottle or not, they'd turn their head when they'd had enough.

It's all about listening to the cues within your body. If you're tired, you sleep. If you need to pee, you pee! Can you imagine being told you have to wait to pee because it's only been two hours since you last went to the bathroom? And yet we do this with food all the time. How can I possibly be hungry if I ate a little while ago? But think about it, particularly for those who menstruate, our cycle affects hunger. What if you worked out really hard this week? You need more fuel. There are so many factors that affect our nutritional needs, but whether or not we ate recently is not one to be concerned about.

I'm sure you have a friend or two who has the ability to leave delicious food on their plate because they are full, right? You may think they are superhuman. How could you possibly leave a morsel of cake behind – travesty! As long as they're not doing so as a way of dieting and restricting, then they are likely intuitive eaters. They haven't been trained out of listening to their body's natural responses and hunger cues.

When I say trained, I mean *trained.* The diet industry does a number on us. From an early age, girls are seeing images in magazines, social media and in pop culture that don't represent the average size. If you're over a certain weight you are rarely seen as an object of desire – you're the fat friend (waves hand frantically – I was the fat friend!).

We're told which food groups are 'bad', what's 'good' and how we need to 'earn' that dessert. It's all bullshit. Food is food, if we let it be. It's the diet industry that tries to make food moral or immoral, because if we're constantly battling ourselves to get smaller then they have products and services to sell us. Over the course of our lives, the average American will spend $112,000 on health and fitness, and that's not even talking about groceries. These are the memberships that you never use, diets that fail, scales to make you over analyze each ounce of intake, beauty products to fix a supposed flaw, or clothes that streamline and squish our bods.

There is nothing wrong with eating foods that fuel you and make you feel vibrant. The challenge comes when we're spending more time worried about our weight than we are focused on our careers, goals and ambitions. Folks! We are more than what we weigh. We are badass individuals who can change the world, but we have to stop obsessing over the scale or our muscle mass and start using our innate talents to change this world for the better.

If you find yourself in the category of being obsessed with food, calorie intake, what you weigh and so on, then make your next book purchase be *Intuitive Eating: A Revolutionary Program That Works by Evelyn Tribole and Elyse Resch*. This book will not only change how you think about food, but it will also boost your self-esteem, and I'll be damned if women in particular don't need bucket loads more self-esteem.

There are ten key principles to intuitive eating. I'm not about to rehash the entire book, but I do want to touch on the principles that I find the most powerful.

We've already talked about how when you're hungry… eat! Well, principle number two of intuitive eating is to Honor Your Hunger. This takes time and practice, but they describe a hunger scale and when you ideally should be eating. It's not about adding new diet rules, it's about recognizing that if you allow yourself to get too hungry, you're likely to binge and if you're too full, you'll feel uncomfortable. There is a zone of genius for satisfying your hunger.

Principle number three is to Make Peace with Food. It's about taking away the "good" or "bad" labels so that food is just food. If you learn to listen to your hunger and what you need, you'll start to be attuned to when you are craving green veggies, when you need some protein, and when a bit of chocolate will actually hit the spot.

Like my former self, you've probably identified some foods as off limits. Psychologically, as soon as you say something isn't allowed you start to crave it. By making peace with food everything is allowed, and so it's not that you can never have it again. Eventually that means that certain foods that you never would have allowed in your house can now live there without risk of constant bingeing. The key component is to trust yourself. When you switch the mindset about food, so much opens up for you.

The seventh principle, and last one I'm going to talk about in this book, is to Cope with Your Emotions Without Using Food. This was a big one for me. I had grown up in a household where food went with everything. You were sad, you ate. You were celebrating, you ate. You were tired, you ate. At the end of the day, using food to cope with emotions isn't the worst coping mechanism out there, and so I've been able to make peace with that, but I've had to beef up my toolbox so that it's no longer the only coping mechanism.

What other coping mechanisms could be in your toolbox? Sometimes what we need is a hot shower where we can cry, to journal, to simply allow yourself to sit with your emotions for a few minutes to see what comes up, to move in the fresh air, to talk with a friend, to drink a cup of tea, to do a craft project, etc. Will you still emotionally eat from time to time? Of course, we all do.

Food is emotional and I'll fight anyone who says otherwise. It's so linked to memory and experience that it would be hard to pull them apart. My husband and I love to travel, and as much as I can recount the temples we visited in Thailand, I also remember the incredible mango sticky rice, the sugar cane on a long hike and holy moly the birthday dinner we had in Hoi An. Food isn't just for survival, it is an art form, and it's more than okay to enjoy it. All of this becomes easier when you a) make peace with food, b) honor your hunger and c) have a toolbox of coping mechanisms to lean on

I am still working on this and always will be. But, if you think about it, I'm a thirty-four-year-old woman and I have been conscious of diet culture being a big part of my life since I was eleven years old. I have over twenty years of diet culture programming that needs rewiring. You probably do as well. So, let's not beat ourselves up if intuitive eating takes time. It's not a quick fix, it's not a diet, it's a way of honoring the needs of your body and mind and that isn't an overnight switch, nor should it be.

My final note on food is that when you are constantly stressed, you may in fact hold on to weight. We know that stress creates cortisol, the stress hormone. Cortisol promotes body fat and makes it incredibly difficult to lose weight. I have clients come to me and part of their overall stress is that they are so focused on losing weight. Not only do they have stress at work and maybe even at home, but then you add weight loss as a goal on top of it and the stress is always with them. Once you're able to stop stressing about weight loss and remove anxiety from other areas of your life, you might find that your body responds in new ways. I'm not guaranteeing it, I'm not promoting it, and I'm not your doctor, but quite often less stress leads to changes in your body be it weight, tension, reduced headaches etc. Begin by listening to what you need and meeting the unmet demands of sleep and nutrition that your body is calling out for.

As you think about the weeks ahead, ask yourself what kinds of foods give you energy? The change you're about to experience is significant, so fuel your body appropriately, whatever that means for you.

Moving Your Body

"Exercise gives you endorphins. Endorphins make you happy. Happy people just don't kill their husbands," said the infamous Elle Woods in Legally Blonde and I can't sum it up any better. But what kind of exercise? How much? What time of day is best? Honestly, it's whatever raises your heart rate. The intensity level of exercise is subjective based on your current fitness level, weight, endurance, etc. You and I could have the exact same body composition, yet react to the same workout differently.

As long as you're in a moderate intensity workout, you're boosting endorphins. Moderate intensity is when you're working to 50-70% of your maximum heart rate. Now I bet you're not bringing a heart rate monitor with you wherever you go, so it's when your breathing quickens but you can still carry on a conversation and you might start sweating. If you increase that to a vigorous exercise, you are breathing heavily and it would be hard to say more than a couple of words. At this intensity you are definitely sweating, and that's because you're operating at 70-85% of your maximum heart rate.

How long does it take to start feeling the effects of exercise on our mood? Studies show that you can see benefits in as little as five minutes[1]. Given that we live in an instant gratification society, five minutes is pretty dang good. People turn to TV, social media, smoking, food or alcohol as a coping mechanism, and while those also have instant effects, they don't last. That's where exercise has a leg up… pun not intended.

Let's talk about some serious shifts that exercise can make on mood, namely those who suffer from depression. In studies conducted at Duke University, sedentary adults with major depressive disorders were divided into four groups and assigned the following treatments: supervised exercise, home-based exercise, antidepressants or a placebo pill. The findings showed that exercise was on par with the antidepressants in terms of remission rates. And you'll find many people anecdotally rave about the power of movement. I've heard people talk about exercise as their church, their medicine or therapy. Let me be clear, exercise is not a substitute for medication if you need medication. Talk to your doctor about this. In my opinion, exercise is part of your mental health and stress management, but it's one piece of the puzzle.

If you tend to suffer from anxiety and/or panic attacks, movement can be immensely powerful. When we're feeling anxious, our limbic system (reptilian/primal brain) is fired up which puts us into fight, flight or freeze. None of those modes are particularly helpful for us when we're not fighting a wild animal. Once you begin moving your body and raising your heart rate, that triggers the parasympathetic nervous system which allows your body to rest and digest by slowing your heart rate, relaxing muscles, your gastrointestinal tract and more.

As I was going through the first three weeks of COVID-19, like everyone reading this, my stress was at an all-time high. My husband's events job vanished, and our day home closed, leaving us home with two toddlers. A huge uncertainty about how we would pay our mortgage in the months to come filled the space like air. I regularly found my heart racing, my body vibrating with tension. The one thing that helped above all else? Moving my body. On some days I managed high intensity workouts and on others it was a walk in the fresh air, but as long as my heart rate was elevated through movement in some way, it helped calm my system for a couple of hours at least.

The other benefit of exercise is that it tends to help people switch off their daily stressors and worries because they have to focus on the task at hand. Think about a yoga class – you are focused on breathing through the movements and moving your body through sometimes challenging positions. It's near impossible to focus on your taxes and yoga class at the same time.

So, as you look at Week Zero and the weeks to come, ask yourself how you are currently moving your body, and if there are ways you want to incorporate more movement. Move your body for five minutes every day. If you desire to move more, incredible, but that five minutes will do wonders for your mental health.

Principle #2: Honesty

Have you ever been working towards a goal alongside someone who was helping you or checking in along the way? Was there a time when things went a little off track? Maybe you didn't meet your word count when writing a book, or you skipped a workout, or you had that drink. And instead of telling that person who was supporting you the truth, you told them what they wanted to hear?

Maybe even what *you* wanted to hear? The sanitized version of things?

I have.

Most of us have.

In this program, because so much of it is done solo and through journal reflections, it is absolutely critical that you be honest with yourself. When you have a hard week, that's okay. Write it out. Talk about it with someone. It's critical that you don't see that bad week as a reason to quit, because that's the opposite of what you need to see transformation.

Often in those moments when we have a challenging week, we make it personal. *I am bad. I suck. I'm no good at this. What was I thinking? I can't do this.* We write this whole narrative in our heads about how things aren't going to change and therefore we quit.

That's not the truth. The truth is IT is hard. The truth is you will get thrown curveballs. The truth is that change takes way more time than we tend to anticipate. The truth is everybody stumbles. And that's okay. Did you notice in all of that truth, not once did I say that *you* are the problem or that *you* are destined to fail? Absolutely not. Why? Because it's not the truth.

Each week in your journal as you're reflecting on wins of the week, challenges that you faced and your plans for the week ahead, ask yourself this question, "Is that true?" Human beings are great storytellers, so make sure that while you're doing the journal work, you're not spinning a tale. Be honest with yourself about what you're feeling. You will go further and faster in this program if you can show up as authentically as possible. You're not doing this for anybody but yourself, so take the time to really get to know you. I'm willing to bet that you've got years of experience burying your truth and your needs in order to show up for the world in a way that was acceptable to others. Start being acceptable to yourself by first accepting yourself, honestly, with no judgement.

Principle #3: Incremental Gains

"Small hinges swing big doors."
~ W. Clement Stone

While we're having the conversation about doing this for yourself, let's also note that your progress and your gains in this program are personal. I do not expect you to pull off an Evel Knieval stunt ride up a steep ramp and over twenty school buses. This isn't about going from total stress ball to Zen monk on a mountaintop, and if that's your expectation you should probably put this book down. I'm not asking you to do the impossible. I'm asking you to show up and focus on small, incremental gains.

Incremental gains, layered one over top of the other become huge change in the long run. More importantly, incremental gains are sustainable. Maybe this week it's about getting consistent sleep. Perhaps that doesn't feel like such a big deal, but next week you add in setting a boundary with your boss, and suddenly things are lightening up a little at work. Then the week after that you shift your mindset about that mother-trucking to-do list and its role in your life. All of a sudden, these micro shifts are leading to bigger and bigger change.

It's easy for me to say that, but I know what most of us are like. If it doesn't *feel* like a big enough shift right away, we view it as failure. Sometimes things actually go down before they come back up. Positive Parenting Educator, Amy McCready, warns parents who take her course that when you shift your parenting techniques to be more calm, supportive and spending more time with your kids, you might actually get more kick-back and misbehavior from them in the early days. I know, I witnessed this and it was one heck of a shock. Kids don't know whether or not to trust the change that is happening, so it's that last push of the buttons to see if you really mean it.

The same goes for adults – it's called self-sabotage. Things start going well, you see small wins and see some light at the end of the tunnel and then suddenly you take actions, consciously or unconsciously, to limit your own success. We will talk all about self-sabotage in Week Five, so we're not going to dive headlong into that now, but what I want to flag for you in the early weeks (and throughout this whole program) is to focus on the small wins. **Each week in your journal I'll ask you what your WTWs are – Wins This Week**. They can be anything and everything that is meaningful to you. Nobody is reading it and judging it. I'd much rather you include more, even if you think they are tiny achievements, rather than have you self-edit and criticize your own progress. Write it all down.

By writing it all down, you'll have a record of evidence, and I guarantee that will come in handy in your low moments. We have a tendency to remember the negative, so by recording your WTWs you can begin to see the entire picture more accurately.

How much do you expect of yourself in a single day or a single week? Probably a lot. You think you can achieve all the tasks on your to-do list, while crushing it at work, while squeezing in self-care and being a kick-ass partner/parent/friend/family member at the same time. Wow, that's a lot on one person's plate for a day or a week.

Get macro. By writing down the micro of the day to day, it allows you to pull back to a macro level and have line of sight on the change and wins you've had over time. When you get to Week Twelve and you look back on all the wins you've had, I guarantee you'll be proud. Because when you add it all up, regardless of if one week was more challenging than another, it's the big picture that will matter. Don't let your feeling of progress come down to one part, one action, one moment in time.

Before you go any further, I want you to grab a sticky note or a piece of paper and tape. Got it? Good. Write down *incremental gains* or *small wins* or something similar and place that somewhere you're going to see it and be reminded of it daily.

Principle #4: Consistency Above All Else

"Success doesn't come from what you do occasionally, it comes from what you do consistently."
~ Marie Forleo

Those incremental gains don't mean anything if you don't show up consistently. Your consistency in this program will be the difference between being significantly less stressed in ninety days versus closing the book at Week Four.

Get rid of the idea of doing this perfectly. There is no such thing. Give yourself permission to show up as the less than best version of yourself, in order to keep putting one foot in front of the other. There is no grade at the end of this, no certificate, no trophy. You will truly get out of this program what you put into it.

I say show up for yourself as though it's easy. It's not. As the Queen of Vulnerability, Brené Brown says, "Sometimes the bravest and most important thing you can do is show up." How do you get consistent about showing up? You'll have to experiment with this, because we are all motivated by different things. In Week One we're going to dive deep into the *why* for your committing to this program. If it's strong enough, like a nine out of ten important to you, you'll do it. If it's not as strong? This may not be the right time for you.

What's powerful about that why is that it's one major goal that you're working towards. The how will include different action items and mechanisms, but we're focusing on one major goal which allows you to stay focused.

Here are some key things to keep in mind as you're building your consistency in stress management, new habits and mindsets:

- **Focus on the process, not the results.** Change happens over time, so if you expect to be Zen after a week, you'll lose motivation and quit. Focus on the habits and the actions you set for yourself each week and see completing them as the success, regardless of the overall outcome. The outcome will happen, give it time to grow.

- **Your old story doesn't define your future.** Just because you've "never" done this before or you've "always" quit on yourself does not mean this is the case now. It's going to be never or always until you flip the script. You aren't your old self any more than you are your future self. You are here. You are now. What matters is how you show up today.
- **Visual cues.** We'll talk in Week One specifically about anchors, but in the meantime, start thinking about what some visual reminders could be for *why* you are invested in this change. They go a long way to keeping you on track when you're in need of a pick me up.
- **Rewards in line with your goal.** I am not opposed to rewards. Does a star sticker chart float your boat? Do it. What's your reward for getting halfway through the program? All the way? Know what that reward is in advance, but make sure it's in line with your overall goal. By that I mean don't pick something that will unknowingly add more stress, rather than take it away. Don't set a goal to be vegan for six weeks and then reward yourself with a juicy steak. Make sure they align.

Consistency takes practice and time. One foot in front of the other.

So, there you have it.

CHIC
C – Core Needs
H – Honesty
I – Incremental Gains
C – Consistency

These are the foundations to prepare for a major transformation in your life. It sounds like a lot, but again, take it one step at a time. Throughout Week Zero, ask yourself what micro-shifts you could make to meet your basic needs for sleep, nutrition and movement. Reflect on whether you're ready to get honest with yourself, regardless of whether that looks shiny and clean or not. Commit to focusing on the incremental gains, the small wins rather than the big gestures. Above all, make the goal to show up consistently.

If you want to take stock of where you're at and capture some early thoughts as you head into this program, head to stresslessin90days.ca to download the journal questions.

You're here for a reason. Let's make this count.

WEEK ONE

WHAT WOULD YOU WALK 500 MILES FOR?

THERE IS A LITTLE OLD SONG BY THE PROCLAIMERS THAT TOPPED charts around the world, where when you hear it, you can't help but sing along and stamp your feet. "I would walk five hundred miles, and I would walk five hundred more, to be the man who walks a thousand miles to fall down at your door." The Proclaimers, a quirky Scottish twin duo, hit on something deeply personal – desire. The feeling when you want something so badly, you'd go to wild lengths to get it.

We often know what we want but do we take the time to understand why we want it? People always ask you what you want. We're used to that. What do you want to be when you grow up? In order for you to have success, not just in this program, but in any other major change or goal in your life, it's important to know the why, and how to build the mechanisms to achieve that why.

First things first, **why does your why matter?**

Viktor Frankl was an Austrian psychotherapist, neurologist and a Holocaust survivor of four concentration camps, including

Auschwitz. His experience was as brutal as we can all imagine. He lost almost all of his family, including his wife, his parents, and his brother. His sister had the luck to escape to Australia.

Following the war, Frankl returned to Vienna where he wrote his well-known book, *Man's Search for Meaning,* in nine days.

He described his observations. He told how the people who seemed most likely to survive concentration camps often didn't. In the end, he found that it didn't come down to who was physically stronger, had more willpower or was more charismatic. The survivors tended to be those who were able to hold onto their faith of freedom, and had some goal or purpose to work towards. For Frankl, writing *Man's Search for Meaning* was that goal.

Frankl had lost the people most important to him, and yet he had a purpose to strive for even on the hardest of days in the camp. "Those who have a 'why' to live, can bear with almost any 'how'" said Frankl.

Resilience research studies our ability to recover from challenging times and backs this up. Researchers have confirmed that one of the keys to resilience is a strong goal or purpose.

Now, our current day struggles are not that of Nazi concentration camps. But our current challenges are valid. The older I get and the more I dive deep with clients, the more I realize how much trauma the average person is carrying around unseen. Abuse, sexual assault, living paycheque to paycheque, chronic illness, racism, loss, harassment, divorce, being laid off, being cheated on, leaving your country of origin… I mean the list is endless.

And if you're reading this book and haven't experienced any of what I've just listed, don't feel guilty about that either - guilt doesn't help anybody. Stress and hardship come in so many forms and intensities, but what ultimately matters is how they affect you and how you are reacting to them. I'm making an educated guess that no matter your particular stressors you're wanting to reduce them, with the hope of something more.

So first, what's your end goal?

Less stress, obviously, but what does that look like? If you picture your life ninety days from now, what does that look like? It's three months, so many of the big markers of your life like your job, relationship, place you live, etc., those may not change (perhaps they will). So, what is realistic? If you've never run a day in your life before, running a marathon in ninety days is hardly realistic. A good rule of thumb is whatever your current state is, plus ten percent improvement.

It's also not about setting goals for things that are outside your control. We can't control other people, the economy, the weather or if we'll win the lotto. We can, however, set goals within ur control by focusing on our habits, a shift in mindset, our boundaries, etc. In these areas, by following the *Stress Less in 90 Days* process and staying accountable, you can definitely see a positive shift in ninety days.

So, what is it that you *really* want? Frame it in the positive. Instead of talking about what you don't want (a horrible boss), focus on what you do want (strong workplace boundaries) as in *I want x* instead of *I don't want y*. If I tell my five-year-old "Don't touch the cookies," you and I both know how that's going to end. When we say *I want such and such* or we praise the positive, our brain looks for evidence and actions to reinforce this.

So, what does your life look like in ninety days? What's different? Who are you spending more time with? What activities are you doing? From the outside, how would I know you're on the right path?

Now, let's figure out the deep down why.

You have your goal. You have a vision for three months from now. Now to figure out the how, we have to answer the why. How we do a thing is fueled by why we do it. You want to stress less. Why? So you perform better at work? Or maybe you want to be more present with your loved ones? Do you simply want to relax in your downtime?

Whatever your 'so that [insert the answer]' is, next I'm going to prod you with the question that tends to stump most people: why is *that* important?

Didn't see that coming, did you? You thought there was one *why*.

Why is it important that you perform better at work or that you're present with loved ones? Maybe something comes to mind right away like how it would help you get a promotion or because you want to not feel distracted with family all the time.

Why is THAT important? What's the "I would walk a thousand miles" reason for your why?

I want you to ask yourself "why is that important" about five or six times. Go down layer by layer, onion style, until you get to the a-ha, oh-that's-it, click into place moment. The click moment is when you understand deep down why your goal is important. For example, at first you may think your goal is to have thirty minutes a day of personal time, but your deep down why is because that makes you feel more connected to yourself, it helps you feel fulfilled by doing a certain hobby, or it makes you feel like the best version of yourself. The click isn't scientific, it's a feeling and you'll know it when you feel it.

This is where the magic happens in understanding your true end game, not just at the end of ninety days, but in general.

Feelings Matter

How do you want to feel?

A mainstay of the corporate world is the concept of having SMART goals (Specific, Measurable, Attainable, Realistic, Timely). This is no shade to SMART goals. I've set them, I've achieved them. I bet you've even set yourself some big goals, but perhaps when you crossed them off, they didn't quite meet your expectations in the same way you'd hoped from the get-go. You didn't feel the click.

This is because SMART goals lack a critical element - how do you want to feel? You probably have an idea of how you want to feel, but if you're not monitoring your feelings as a key indicator of whether you're on the right track or not, then you are very likely to get to your end goal and feel dissatisfied.

Whhhhhhhhy?

Because satisfaction is a damn feeling.

Think about it. Many of us don't strive to get married so that we can sign a piece of paper and share our worldly belongings with another person - we do it because we want to feel connection. Runners don't work their butt off to train for a marathon just to glory in all the blisters and bleeding toe nails at the end of it. They're striving for that runner's high, the overwhelming feeling of crossing the finish line, knowing they've pushed themselves to the limit and come out the other end. We don't move houses, cities or countries to enjoy the process of packing boxes, dealing with realtors and facing a new job hunt. We do it because we feel it's going to provide something...more. More opportunities. More new experiences. More options.

The feeling is absolutely critical. Without it, it's not so much a goal than it's a to-do list. A why without strong feeling behind it is a 'so what'?

So WHY is your goal so important to you (the deep down why) and HOW do you want to feel? I'd go a step further and ask how you want to feel in the process of working towards your goal? I bet the answer isn't miserable, and yet I see so many people striving for goals and they are totally downcast and miserable the entire time.

How do you want to feel while working towards your goal? A sense of purpose? Driven? Like you're building energy or peace? You won't feel that every day or in every moment because feelings aren't permanent, but if you're starting to feel glimmers of that feeling grow over time, you know you're on the right track.

We need to know where you're going and what's fueling it. Yes, we can layer in new strategies, tools and mindset shifts to help you stress less that are generalized. They'd give you some relief. But if you want real and meaningful change in your life you need to be clear on how, when and why you want to stress less. You need to know what you want to do with all that extra energy you're going to free up. The 'so what or so that' is what you're doing with that extra energy. The deep down why puts the fire in your belly to get there.

Gut Check

On a scale of 1-10, how important is this goal to you? If you're sitting at an eight or higher, then it's the right goal for you to tackle. Anything less than that and I bet you're going to lose steam and not prioritize it.

We tend not to make changes when we're comfortable. The stakes aren't high enough. But you define the stakes. What's an eight for me and an eight for you will be different, but so long as it's important to you, you'll get there with the right road map.

So, take some time to really flesh this goal (or goals) out. Don't rush it. Take the time and really dig into your why and you'll see the difference.

I often have people ask me if their goal is "good enough" or "right". There's no such thing. My golden rule is that as long as it doesn't cause pain to anyone else or yourself, and it's important to you, it's your goal. Discomfort… discomfort is okay, because that's where growth happens. Pain signals to me we're not on the right path with your goal. Be honest about the difference with yourself.

Shoring Up Your Why

You know your deep down why. Awesome. Not to put too fine a point on it, but you're going to lose sight of it at some point along this journey. We all do. So, before the going gets tough, let's shore up the foundation of your why so it can handle a couple hard knocks.

Find Your Anchors

An anchor is something in your physical environment that acts as a pattern interrupt to remind you of your goal. Why is this important? Because when we take on new habits or mindsets, it's easy for us to fall back into the status quo. Humans like the status quo. Our prehistoric ancestors weren't worried about personal development, they were worried about survival and preserving energy for when they'd need it next. The status quo feels safe, comfortable and certain.

Goals and status quo aren't bedfellows, so to get out of your routine, you'll need constant reminders of why you're working towards your desired state. We need reminders in order to be consistent. Anchors do that.

Anchors come in all shapes and sizes. Maybe it's a mantra that you write on sticky notes around the house, or a piece of jewelry that you infuse with some meaning. Remember when people used to wear elastic bands around their wrist to remind them not to forget something? Same idea. If you drive everywhere, perhaps it's something hanging from your rear-view mirror. Someone constantly working from their laptop and phone, might use a screensaver as an anchor.

Brendon Burchard is a high-performance coach and author of *High-Performance Habits*, and at one stage in his life he wanted to shift his habitual mindset to bringing joy to every area of his life. If that hasn't been your default, how are you going to constantly remember to do that? For Brendon it was doorways. Each time he walked through a doorway, he'd tell himself to *bring the joy*. A doorway was a pattern interrupt that would be with him wherever he went.

I had a rough go of my first pregnancy. I contracted shingles from stress, there were layoffs at work, and my parents were unexpectedly getting divorced. I was unbelievably stressed, and I often wondered how I was going to make it through. I knew I needed to pull on my inner reserves both for myself and for my baby.

I bought a Giving Key (a super cool social enterprise out of the U.S.) with the word "strength" inscribed on it. I wore that necklace every day for the last trimester. When I was feeling low and drained, I grabbed onto it and practically squeezed as hard as I could. That key was a constant reminder of what I needed, what I was working towards and how it would all be okay on the other side. During the worst moments of my delivery I grabbed onto that key. In the months that followed, when the need for physical strength gave way to mental and emotional demands, I grabbed onto that key. It was my anchor.

Look around you. What anchors will help you interrupt your day-to-day life and remind you to keep working towards your desired state? Find one, find many. But take some time to really imbue them with meaning so they no longer feel like everyday objects.

Setting Action Items

Each week my clients and I set action items that get them one step closer to their goals. Step is the operative word. It's not about giant shifts in action. We can all make sweeping gestures and commitments, only to later falter. The best plan is to make tangible, achievable micro moves towards your goals. You know, steps. For Week One in particular, make it an action item so easy you know you'll smash it. We need to build momentum and faith in yourself that you can follow through consistently.

Knowing your goal and your deep down why, next I want you to ask yourself what is an action you can take this week that is realistic? Have you been putting something off?

This is your week. Do it.

Remove the Obstacles

Spoiler alert - just because you've set a goal doesn't make it a slam dunk to achieve - otherwise you'd have already done it. You're going to face obstacles, whether outside of yourself or in your own head and heart. **How are you going to make it inevitable?** How are you going to make it so that even with obstacles in your way, you will still achieve your goals? What are you going to do to ensure that this time you follow through? This is why I never shame people for not achieving their goals: one, because that would make me an asshole lacking empathy and two, because most people have never thought about how to proactively remove obstacles in their way. I never did. If you aren't, you might still achieve your goals without acknowledging the obstacles in your way and removing them but it'll be like trying to run on a pebbled beach instead of grass.

What are the obstacles in your way? Some will be outside obstacles: a person, an event, a location, a time restraint, etc. Others are entirely in our heads: how you feel about something, how you judge your self-worth, motivation, energy levels, etc. Obstacles come in all forms, all shapes and sizes and hit differently for everyone.

People often block our progress. They disagree with us, don't allow us certain opportunities or they actively work to sabotage us. Think of women and people of color being denied the vote for so long - it was people who tried to block their way. If a person is blocking your progress, you have to decide how you're going to deal with it whether it be going around them, collaborating, talking through it and moving forward, spending less time with them or whichever approach best serves your situation.

If an event or a period of time is going to make it harder for you to achieve your goals, think through the variables. COVID-19 is a perfect example. It has made it harder for many of us to achieve our goals be they health, financial, relationships or otherwise. In response, we need to find a new way around. Take parenting during COVID for example - parents have had a rough go of it trying to figure out how to be their child's teacher while showing up at their own full-time job online or in person. Many of them are squeezing their work into the wee hours of the morning, burning themselves out. So, what's the solution? Well, that's the thing - there's no one-size fits all for any of us. Can you talk to your boss about expectations? Can you lower your own expectations of yourself as your child's teacher (hey, you didn't train to do this, it's okay if you're not perfect!)? Can you embrace the messiness and stop trying to make it something it's not? Can you have a family meeting to look for alternatives? I know one parent whose child learns better in the evening, so they embraced that. Is that the typical school day? No, but it works for his peak energy and it allows his parents to work during the day while he keeps himself busy with other activities, including sleeping - ah to be a teenager.

My point is that events and seasons of life will throw us off kilter. It's okay to take the time you need to get the lay of the land. Once you find some semblance of normal, that's when you've got the brainpower to problem solve. And remember, you're not problem solving based on anyone else's criteria of success except your own. This is highly personal.

Now what about the challenges swirling around inside your mind? The monkey mind can be devilish. One minute it has you thinking you're a rock star for an accomplishment and the next it has you doubting yourself, your skills, your worthiness.

What can be helpful is to recognize the mental patterns that you regularly experience. More likely than not, these swirling thoughts probably pop up based on a trigger. Can you brainstorm on what that would be? For me, whenever I go clothes shopping, the swirl begins. I've been all kinds of weights and sizes, but body dysmorphia is real and will have me thinking that nothing fits, I'm ugly, that I should just give up, etc. So now, knowing that this would happen almost every time I'd go to buy clothes, I change the pattern. I preemptively tell myself I'm beautiful, that if the clothes don't look right it's that piece of clothing and not me, and I tie some sort of reward to the experience like a phone call with a friend or a favorite audiobook to listen to on my way home. As a result, I get what I need, I don't indulge in negative self-talk and I have a much better time.

So, what is your pattern? What's the cue? What change of state are you looking for? What different action could you take to get there? What obstacle can you remove?

Remember to Stay Accountable

You need to be accountable to someone if you want to amplify your progress. Who will you be accountable to? Let them know your goals, tell them you'll check in with them at 'x' time each day or week, and ask them to hold you to it. Also, tell them why this is important to you. You're both more likely to stick to it when you've reiterated why this goal has soul beneath it.

I'm not going to wish you luck this week, because luck assumes that you aren't playing a major role in making this happen. I'm going to wish you good energy and strong conviction. You've got this. Now go take the first step of your five hundred miles.

Recap

- You are much more likely to achieve goals when you know the deep down why. Get clear on it.
- How you want to feel is just as important as 'what' you want to experience.
- Anchors keep our why top of mind and act as a pattern interrupt in hard moments.
- Proactively planning and removing obstacles makes it easier to achieve your weekly action items.

Head to the workbook for this week's journal exercises at stresslessin90days.ca.

WEEK TWO
ALIGN YOUR ENERGY

DID YOU EVER PLAY WITH MAGNETS AS A KID? I LOVED TESTING their polarity and feeling the sensation of the opposite poles pulling together and snapping in place. It was also a fun game to see how close you could get the same poles together, feeling them pushing away from one another despite me trying to make them touch.

Your mental and emotional energy is not that dissimilar to the push and pull of magnets. When your actions, schedule, activities, etc. align with your values, you snap into place. It takes less effort, it's easier and it's a satisfying "click". Conversely, when you're engaged in activities that you don't align with, you and that activity (be it cleaning your home, doing that project at work or spending time with someone you dread) are those magnets repelling off of one another. It's hard, it's draining and there is certainly no satisfaction of snapping into place. Alignment matters.

What do I even mean by being in alignment? Being in alignment is when your actions, words and activities are in congruence with the values that you hold.

Let's unpack that.

If you've never taken time to think through your values, these are the things that are most important to you. These are the things that are the core of what matters to you, and when you're feeling off, or like something is rubbing you the wrong way, I'm willing to bet a value is being compromised.

In Week Zero we talked about how to meet your core needs: sleep, nutrition and movement. These build your physical energy which you need to move forward with any goal. In Week One you uncovered your deep down why so that you have a guiding north star throughout this program. Our why manifests as values, but you need clarity on your values in order to get alignment, which strengthens your mental and emotional energy which you need in large supply to achieve any goal. Strong values help you make better decisions, show up for yourself and others, and shed regret.

What Do You Value?

When it comes to values, most people spout off mainstays like health, friendship and family. Sure, those are important, but do you actually value them? You know they're important, but do you *value* them? If you really value them, you'll begin showing up in a bigger way.

So, let's uncover your values. First off, I want you to get out a sheet of paper, or you can also find this activity in the workbook at stresslessin90days.ca. We're going to start by reviewing some of the highlights of your life. Scroll back and think of the peaks in your personal history. Getting a certain job? A travel experience? The birth of a child? Buying your home? Confirming your gender? Starting a business? Graduating from school? It truly doesn't matter what they are, how big or how small, what matters is whether or not they stick out to you.

Once you list a few of these moments, I want you to put them under a microscope. What was it about these moments that was special? Who was there? What do those moments or accomplishments represent to you? How did they impact your life going forward? Did they change you?

I know, I know, I've thrown a lot of questions at you, so this is a good time to put this book down and do the work. Pick it back up when you're done.

(Stop reading this - go do the work!)

Okay, you did it!

Now, as you review those moments are you seeing any trends? Can you draw any conclusions from what was important about them to you and assign a value to it? Note that in your workbook you also have a long list of values - you don't need to care about them all, but see which ones resonate and perhaps tie to those peak moments.

For me, one highlight has been launching my business, Stress Less Ladies. It's given me proof that there is work that aligns with my values where I can make a positive impact on people and it's on my own terms. Being an entrepreneur gives me the flexibility to run my life as I like it. This doesn't mean it's not full of hard work, but I feel aligned.

You know that saying where if you find a job you love, you won't work a day in your life? Well, it's a bit bullshit, because I most definitely hate doing my bookkeeping and slogging through emails, but it's about the energy involved. If you love your work, if you're in alignment with it, there are plenty of instances where it will add to your energy instead of pull from it.

Now, I write this particular section as I've just accepted a new full-time job outside of Stress Less Ladies. I won't lie, I have concerns. My concern is that this job will rub against my value of flexibility. Valid concern.

But then consider that another one of my values is security. I have two young kids and above everything I want to ensure their basic needs are provided for and that they never have to worry about where their next meal is going to come from. This trumps my desires as an entrepreneur (for now). So, as we move to another province to start our new phase of life, the value of stability is taking the front seat.

Values can do this. We can value many things, but not get to experience each one of them in full form simultaneously. Sometimes values conflict. For right now, I'll let flexibility take a back seat, continue to run my business and take on a full-time job that brings my family the stability we need to live the quality of life we desire. It's a balancing act.

Negative experiences also factor into our values. I remember when I was young people would ask me what I wanted to be when I grew up. I could list a bunch of things, but have no clear direction. But ask me what I did NOT want to do and I had a very concrete list. I had zero desire to be a nurse, not because it's not a valuable profession (I love nurses!), but because bodily fluids make me gag. That last piece is at odds with raising toddlers, that's for sure.

Reflect on some of the hardest moments in your life. I know this isn't the fun part, but it is important. When you look at those moments that stick out as the worst, what was it about them that made it that way? Who was there? What was happening? What was the impact? How did it make you feel? Take a minute to write down your answers to these, then come back to me.

You're back. That might have been difficult, dredging up things you'd rather have left in the shadows. I get it. But were there common themes? By knowing what you don't want to experience, you can then look at the opposite. If you don't want rigidity, you want flexibility. If you don't want disrespect, you want respect. If you don't want to be closed off, you want open communication. You get the drift.

Take a few minutes and reflect on both the highest and the lowest moments, review your findings and write down the three to five values that come to the forefront.

We are many-layered people, so you likely have more than five things that you value, but when push comes to shove there will be a rare few that are more important than others.

I suggest revisiting this exercise every few years or as new life events occur. My values now are different to before kids, they've changed with age, with careers and with loss. COVID-19 also shifted my values for the time being, as I'm sure you've experienced in your own life. We're meant to grow and evolve, so just because something is of value to you now doesn't mean it will be forever. Reassess your values periodically.

Flesh It Out

Now that you have your three to five values, it's important to flesh them out so that you know how they can and will show up in your daily life. Ask yourself some pointed questions:

- If I'm living out the value of [insert value here] my life will look like...
- If I'm living out the value of [insert value here], my calendar will look like...
- An outsider looking in would know that I value [insert value here], because they see me...
- The biggest obstacle in my current life to this value is...
- I will work around this obstacle by...

Answer these questions for each value. It's one thing to say something is a value, it's another thing entirely for it to show up in how you think, what you say, the activities that you do, etc.

My biggest value is my time. When I'm living out my value of time, I'm working smarter and not harder. I'm looking for efficiencies, I'm not late for meetings, and I carve out the time I need not only to be productive, but to be a good parent, a good partner and have time to rest and refuel.

If I'm living out this value, my calendar looks well-organized. I rarely work overtime, because I prioritize appropriately and aim to do the hard things first each day so that I'm not procrastinating.

An outsider looking in would know that I value my time because

I am never late for a meeting, I am efficient, I come prepared and I safeguard my weekends and evenings for my family.

The biggest obstacle in my current life to this value is honestly myself. It would be so easy to say yes to things that I'd rather say no to. I need strong boundaries to ensure that I don't let other people take the time that I need and crave. I also need to ensure that I'm not saying yes when I would rather say no, that I am continuously prioritizing so I'm not wasting hours on busy work, and I develop systems and routines to improve efficiency. We'll talk about each of these and more throughout the program.

I work around this obstacle by constantly honing and tweaking when I go off course. I schedule breaks. I know in my bones when I feel connected and aligned, as opposed to hurried and rushed - I most definitely prefer one state over the other.

I'm not going to live out this value perfectly. You're not going to live out your values perfectly. The question is **are you in alignment more often than not?**

Now that you know your values and you've fleshed out what they look like, you can aim for alignment.

Values as Decision Drivers

If someone asks you where you want to go for dinner or what movie you want to go see, do you have an answer right away or do you hum and haw and see what they want to do? Do you spend hours online researching the crap out of any purchase?

Decision fatigue is the deteriorating quality of our decision-making after a prolonged period of making decisions. We make decisions all day long and it can drain our energy and add stress. We'll talk more about this in Week Eight, but for now, decisions big and small can be made much more easily when you use your values as your decision-making criteria. When you know your values (write them down, keep them somewhere obvious), they can be your guide to making strong, no-looking-back decisions.

Applying for a new job? Use these values to determine if it's the right fit for you. Ask questions to get a better sense of how this job fits with your values when you're in the interview process.

Starting a new relationship, be it friendship, family or romantic - are you living out your values with that person and are they respecting your values? If you value continual growth but your partner wants to stay put and doesn't believe in personal development it's not impossible for it to work, but you're going to have tension points for sure. To be clear, you and your partner certainly do not need to be mirror images of each other. The question is **do they respect your value and give you the space to live it out?** Or are they actively getting in your way and detracting from your value? If it's the latter, then there's a problem.

I value my mental health. After significant burnout, anxiety and depression, I do not want to purposely put myself on the path to experience these again. It may still happen, but I don't want to be the creator of it. So, I'm constantly looking at all the ways to care for my mental health from how I move my body to what I eat, how much sleep I get to seeking out help when needed. When I'm tired, I rest. When I need help, I ask for it. I give myself grace that not everything works out all the time and I'm allowed to screw up. And I regularly recalibrate when my toddlers have been non-stop screaming and ignoring my directions for hours. Recalibrating your emotions is about noticing when things are getting too intense (you're too tired, mad, sad, overly excited, etc.) so that you can bring yourself back to a more neutral state that allows you to do what you want and need to do. Being in alignment with your values helps keep you calibrated.

My mental health is at the forefront when I'm making decisions. Will this choice negatively or positively impact my mental health? Or is it a net-neutral? If it's going to impact me negatively, is there something else I can do to counteract that? Because, truth be told, there are times when we have to make a choice that will have an adverse effect on a value we hold dear.

I don't know anyone who enjoys the process of moving. Moving is extremely stressful. In the fall of 2020, my partner and I packed up our house, sold it during the freaking global pandemic, had to keep the house clean for viewings with a two year old and a four year old... and that was before we moved to a new province and stayed in temporary accommodation while we searched for our next home. It took a toll on my mental health. But we had to do all of these things, because on the other side of the move was the quality of life we were striving for.

So, what do we do? We counteract, increasing self-care where possible. We adjust expectations and create systems to support us through hard times. To minimize decision making we create routines. Where we can, budget permitting, we outsource. But what about the small decisions? I see clients living out their values in big decisions, but it's the small, everyday interactions where I see the erosion of what matters to them. They say yes to a commitment they don't care about. They let someone treat them in a way they don't like. They don't speak up in meetings. They don't take time for the things that matter to them. These small, seemingly insignificant moments are where you can change the game one move at a time.

This week I want you to put on your detective hat and observe where you are living out of alignment in both big and small ways. What are those little decisions you make (or don't make) that are counter to what you value? Then ask yourself what you can do differently next time and how you'll make it inevitable.

Remember, you're likely eroding your values because it's easier in the moment, but easier in the moment can lead to pain in the long run. What is one little way you can re-align this week? This entire program is about those small, micro shifts to get to where you want to be long-term. Make it achievable. Commit to it, plan for it, do it, then reflect on the impact of this change. And celebrate! Even if it's one small thing you did differently, celebrate that success.

Celebration is so key, because it signals to your brain what actions are worthy of doing again and again. It gives you a kick of dopamine which helps motivate you to repeat the action. Train your brain for what you want to experience. You've probably got years of unlearning to do, so when you take action aligned with your values, recognize it and celebrate.

At the end of the day, like those magnets you'll feel the satisfying click when you're in alignment with your values. Whenever you feel that push back, the "it's just not right" feeling, or like you're actively being repelled, you are out of alignment. Step back, reassess, realign.

Review Last Week

As you look back on the last seven days, I want you to ask yourself **what wins did I have this week?** This is a question you're going to reflect on each and every week and it's mega-important. Too often we gloss over our accomplishments, big or small. We nitpick the challenges and our failures all day long, which shows where we're spending the bulk of our energy. A great way to boost that energy is to realize what has been gaining momentum for you.

Mark these down in your journal as either a weekly reflection or in real time as they're happening. It could be that you got some time to yourself, that you did in fact achieve your action item, that you were able to take more mindful moments and be present, or anything that you deem went well and/or you're grateful for. In the early weeks these lists can be hard to write, but I promise as we go along you'll find the WTW (Wins This Week) list will start to flow.

Recap

- Review high and low moments throughout your life to find clues to the values you hold most dear.
- Identify one way in which you're going to get into alignment with a value this week (be it a task, activity, behavior or a relationship you're going to tweak).
- Outline an action item for this week. Perhaps you're taking last week's action item a step further, or you're

layering a new one on top. Remember, you can set multiple action items, just don't bite off more than is realistic to chew.
- Touch base with your accountability partner.

You've got this.

WEEK THREE

THE "B" WORD

I'M WILLING TO BET THAT IN THE NOT SO DISTANT PAST YOU SAID YES to something you really didn't want to do. Maybe you felt like you had to, there was no choice, you were obligated, or whatever the case may be. This happens. We're never going to be permanently aligned. Adulting often means there are tasks we have to do or conversations to be had that we'd prefer not to. Cleaning my toilet does not make me feel aligned or like my best self! The challenge comes when we're constantly out of alignment.

In Week Two, you did a deep dive into what your personal values are. We talked about how your values can be the best guide when making any decision. Well, your boundaries will be a series of decisions that you need to make for yourself. If you don't, other people will decide for you, and that's a quick way to be frustrated, stressed and dissatisfied with your life.

Boundaries

Stress is reduced when we improve our boundaries. So, what is a boundary? Your boundaries are the set of rules, guidelines or behaviors that you define as reasonable in order to engage with a person or an activity. Note it said that *you* define what is reasonable. My boundaries and your boundaries will look different.

Here's what boundaries are not:

- A brick wall that you never cross
- Never finding compromise
- Cutting people out entirely if you don't agree with them

On that last one, let me be clear that there are certain people who you may choose not to have in your life for very good reasons. It makes sense to have a solid line in place for your safety and stability with the toxic people in your life, the people who have abused you in some way. With the majority of people, however, our lives function better when we learn to compromise while maintaining a firm boundary to back it up.

What does it mean to have a boundary crossed? It can be hard to put your finger on it as a bystander, but when it happens to you, you feel it. It's a feeling of discomfort, of being in a situation or a conversation you don't want to be part of. You might feel betrayed, or you might feel like you pushed yourself and your values to the side in order to meet the needs of others. In that situation you're valuing their needs or desires over your own. You made your boundaries a free-for-all. Drinks on the house!

Are boundaries selfish? Depends on your feelings about the word selfish. The traditional definition of selfish is when you lack consideration of others and are solely concerned with your own needs. The opposite of selfish would be selfless, in which you are only concerned with the needs of others. Neither one is fantastic, but if I'm going to pick one, I'd rather be selfish.

Michelle Elman, the author of *The Joy of Being Selfish* explains how selflessness seems like a morally superior way of living, when in fact it serves the selfless person's desire to feel helpful and wanted. So, for them, being selfless is self-serving. Boundaries are about you feeling safe and comfortable - I would hardly call that selfish.

Does a boundary mean that if we disagree with someone, we never engage with them again? In my podcast interview with Komal

Minhas, a producer of the documentary *Dream, Girl* and a resilience educator, she talked about how cutting people out is lazy, and I agree. Not lazy as in a judgement on you, but lazy in that communicating, working and living with people is incredibly hard work and we have to stop expecting it to be easy. We have to stop expecting that we will agree with everyone, that they'll share our world view, or that they will have the same innate set of rules and guidelines to living their lives that we do. There is beauty in our diverse thoughts and upbringings, but that also means we think and behave differently.

If you're still struggling to come up with a boundary, I have four steps to creating a rock-solid boundary. While they seem simple, implementing them takes practice.

1) Define What Is and Isn't Okay Behavior for You.

Isn't it great that we did values work in the last chapter? If a boundary is the guidelines that you define as reasonable, then we have to start by defining reasonable according to you. This may look different depending on the person you're with or the environment that you're in.

For example, with your friends, you might be very open to talking about personal topics like your love life, your family dynamics, politics, etc. In the workplace, on the other hand, those topics might be a no-go zone for you. It could even be different within the same friend group. Maybe you're okay talking with Jenny about your sex life, but not with Cass, because you've had experiences that have broken trust.

There are a few questions to ask yourself. With this person, what am I comfortable discussing or doing? What am I not comfortable discussing or doing? What do I need to feel safe and protected?

Sex is most definitely an area of our lives where we need clear boundaries. It's important to have candid conversations with our partners about what we want and equally what we don't want. What words are we comfortable with, and which upset or trigger us? There should never be an assumption that because something excites you that it has the same effect on the other person. It could be crossing an important personal boundary, and when we're becoming physically intimate with someone, there is a shared responsibility to communicate what is and isn't consensual behavior.

What about in the workplace? How do your values and needs come into play when you're dealing with the dynamics of multiple people: your supervisor, your team members or the culture of your workplace? Maybe your boss always emails you after hours expecting a response. Or perhaps your coworker doesn't respect you wearing headphones as a sign that you don't want to be disturbed. Maybe your team members are perpetually late for meetings and you're trying to finish on time to get home to your dog.

How about boundaries in the digital world? When I started growing my online presence through my blog and social media, my husband and I had a clear conversation about not including our kids' photos on social media. If you scroll back in the archives, you'll find photos of my son every month of his first year, the standard growth photo. Since then, I've tried very hard to only photograph my kids where their faces are out of frame, or I cover their faces with little stickers. It's a boundary that makes my husband and I much more comfortable. Do I judge others who show photos of their kids online? No. I love seeing those photos! But I need to take actions that make myself, my husband and our kids feel safe and respected.

What about your family of origin or the primary people who you grew up with? Woof, this is a big one. Family can both easily trigger and easily ignore our boundaries because they've known us the longest and we've likely had the most casual of relationships with them. Whatever your birth position in the family growing up that can carry over into how you're treated even as a full-grown adult. You get to decide if that treatment is okay for you now or not. You get to decide whether or not you discuss certain topics. You get to decide how to live your life. You get to decide if you need space.

2) Define the Boundary and Consequence if Crossed

One example of a boundary is a legal contract. The majority of people reading this book have rented an apartment or a house. You sign a lease that says that you agree to abide by certain rules and a set monthly payment in exchange for the right to live in that space. You don't make copies of your key without permission, you don't play music after 10 p.m., and you definitely NEVER leave a candle unattended... scratch that, no candles. Only you can prevent house fires.

I'm not suggesting that you write up a contract for each relationship that you're in, but imagine for a second that you were to write a contract for major relationships in your life: your friends, your colleagues, your family, the people you have romantic relationships with. What would your contract say? What are the clauses that you would need for you to feel safe and comfortable in their presence? What would you need in order to feel like your relationship is reciprocal? What would you need to feel like you could thrive alongside that person? Write it all down.

Some common clauses include:

- We agree that if I am feeling tired and frustrated, that I will take some time to myself so that I don't snap and say something regrettable.
- My partner agrees to put the toilet seat down as a sign of respect.
- My boss knows that I won't respond to emails after 5 p.m.
- My friends agree not to be late to get togethers.
- My kids agree not to play in mommy's bedroom, as it's her quiet place.
- My ex has specific times he can come and visit the kids and our pets.
- I don't want to be touched by certain people, but I'm comfortable being touched by specific loved ones.
- I don't loan money.

Your contract will look different to mine because what we are each comfortable with, what we need and what we value all vary. Spice of life right there.

What about the consequences? Go back to that lease. What happens if you start a small fire in your apartment? Does the contract say that they can evict you? Or is there a process of 'x' number of warnings? Spend time with children and you'll see boundaries being created all the time. If you hit your sister, you immediately need to say sorry, and you won't get TV screens for the rest of the day. Clear and concise.

When communicating a boundary and the consequence, it's commonly a "if this, then that" discussion. If you email me after hours, I will not respond until the next business day. If you make comments about my parenting, I will remove myself from the conversation. If you are late for class, the teacher will shut the door and you miss it. If you don't hand in your homework on time, you fail. If you don't clean your toys off the stairs, they will be confiscated. Back to the clauses that you developed above, **what is a reasonable consequence for each one if breached?**

3) To Communicate or Not to Communicate

Is it a requirement that you communicate your boundaries to the other person? Hot topic for sure, but I don't think it's always required to verbalize the boundary. If you're in a situation where you can, do so. As Brené Brown says, "Clear is kind". When you can be clear with your needs and intentions, it helps all parties.

I also recognize that there are other tricky factors at play in real life. Cultural and societal expectations. Age differences. Personal dynamics. Safety. There are layers that make communicating a boundary harder in some situations than in others.

For example, if you have a tenuous relationship with your in-laws, do you need to verbalize your boundary to them? Perhaps not. As long as you're following through with the action that you need to feel safe and comfortable, then do that. Maybe your partner goes to their house for dinner and you stay home this time.

In many cultures, talking back to elders is unheard of, so perhaps in those situations you choose to change your behavior. If a topic is brought up that you don't want to discuss, you excuse yourself, or you provide very little response. Similar to asking a teenager how their day at school was, one-word answers or limited info quickly stalls a conversation. They can't play tennis if you let the ball drop.

Some boundaries may not require any communication at all because it's more about how you respond to a situation. You may not need to respond to emails after hours, but you've made it your norm in the past; change the behavior. You may not need to volunteer for extra projects or community efforts, but you chose to. Adjust your own behavior and choices going forward in order to enforce your own boundary. Say no. "No is a complete sentence," says Anne Lamott.

Should you justify your new boundary? As much as you can, and as challenging as I know it may feel, try *not* to justify your boundary. I get how hard this may be. For years I was the queen of justification. I told friends that I couldn't go out because I had so much work to do, when in reality I was tired, drained or just wanted some beloved introverted time to myself. The amount of times I was probably "sick" or "busy" over the years is just a pile of excuses that even I can't keep straight, and it wasn't fair to lie to my friends. Now I try to simply say no to an event or a commitment with a simple "no thanks" or "it's not a fit for me right now". Then I stop myself from filling in the blanks. The more you try and justify your needs, the less empowered you are.

Now, if you're choosing to communicate the boundary, my suggestion is you practice it out loud first. What is your "if this, then that" boundary? You can even preface it with what you value. Here are some examples:

- I really value my free time. If you aren't on time going forward, then I will leave and go home.
- I don't check emails on vacation / after 5 p.m.
- I don't talk about politics at work. *Then if your coworkers*

start these conversations you can either remind them of your stance, or remove yourself from the conversation. No need to communicate the consequences in this situation.

- If you have an issue with me, please communicate it to me. I don't want to be talked about behind my back.
- (*When you have divorced parents/friends)* I can't talk with you about (other parent/friend).

The variations are endless, but per the previous step it's usually an "if this, then that", or a clear-cut statement of what you will tolerate.

4) Reinforce Your Boundary

If you've had weak boundaries in the past, your friends, family and/or coworkers will have a habit of engaging with you in a certain way. They will more likely cross your boundary, whether out of intentional confrontation or unintentional habit. You need to be prepared for that, and the best way that I know how is through mental rehearsal.

Imagine that the person you're trying to create/enforce a boundary with has crossed it. How will you behave? What will you say? What will your self-talk be so that you don't crumble? Rehearsal isn't about worst-case scenarios as much as it is about preparing you to hold firm. If you haven't had strong boundaries before, it takes some practice.

Similar to how we focus on your weekly goals and action items, ask yourself how you can set yourself up for success. When a boundary is crossed, especially with a newly communicated boundary, having a game plan to manage that puts you in an empowered position.

Where to Start with Boundaries

You might be thinking to yourself that there are so many boundaries in your life that need improvement. If boundaries are new for you, my humble suggestion is that you start with low hanging fruit. True, the boundary change you'll benefit from the most is the biggest one, but that can feel intimidating. Start small, get practice, build confidence, and from there you can layer on stronger and stronger boundaries with more and more impact. What would be the boundary you could create today that would be easy to create? Start with that one, then layer up like a glorious mille feuille pastry.

Boundaries With and For Yourself

Some of the hardest boundaries are the ones you maintain with and for yourself. By this, I mean that you have clearly outlined what you want (your values), and you've identified the behaviors that support that. You might call this a goal or you might call it a personal boundary. For example, a person who values their time with friends and family might have a firm boundary that they finish work at 4 p.m. every day. A person who values their sobriety and the life that it allows them to lead might have a boundary that they do not drink.

You can make more money. You can get more help. You can redo many mistakes. You cannot make more time. We can be incredibly flippant about time, both our own and the time of others. It's not uncommon to see people late for meetings. We see a gap in someone's' calendar and book our slot without thinking if that person will even get a break between meetings that day. We give away the time we planned to spend on an important project in lieu of someone else's needs.

If you don't guard your time, nobody else will. It is fleeting and precious. You can fill it with fluff, or you can use your time to live in alignment with your needs and desires. As someone whose career was once described as fluffy by a colleague, let me clarify that in this case I mean the universal definition of time fluff (in my opinion), which is having your time stolen for activities that feel unfulfilling, unproductive and/or lacking in joy. Something may be unproductive but brings you joy like watching Netflix. Not fluff! Mindless scrolling that you're hoping will fill a void but doesn't?

Fluff. A two-hour meeting that could have been an email? Total fluff.

This week I want you to take a serious look at your schedule or calendar and de-fluff it. Ah... your calendar. Some of us live by it, some of us dread it. At the end of the day, your calendar is a reflection of what matters to you. "I don't have time for..." is a common phrase that I hear and yet clients are filling micro-moments with scrolling social media, gossip, internet surfing, TV, or something that helps them zone out.

There is a place for rest and relaxation, but zoning out usually means you're out of alignment so much of your day that you literally want to escape your brain. It's as though you want to take the memory of the day, pull it out of your head and push it to the side. Pause your brain, cool. Escape your brain... I think we can do better than that in the long run.

Take out your calendar and have a look at all the activities there. One by one, go through and put a check mark next to the activities that align with your values, a dash next to the ones that are neutral, and a cross against the ones that are out of alignment.

What does your calendar look like? If you're not someone who typically tracks their activities on a calendar, for the purposes of this exercise I suggest tracking an average day in fifteen-minute increments. Don't worry, you don't have to do this all the time, but you need to become aware of how you're spending your time so that you can alter what doesn't work.

Okay, now focus on the ones with a cross next to them. What about those activities is out of alignment? Is it work, home, or another commitment? How can you bring it more into alignment, or at a minimum make it neutral? This could look like outsourcing, spending less time on it, delegating it, or simply not doing it at all. Perhaps this is a work commitment and it's just something you have to do. We all have those things - adulting isn't always fun! How can you make the experience less painful? Are there habits you can develop so these things just happen (more on habits in the next chapter)? Is there a way you can tie a reward to doing that activity so you're a little more motivated? Can you break it up, or perhaps batch it so it's done all at once? There are all kinds of ways that we can tweak what we're doing. Just because something has always been done a certain way doesn't mean it has to continue in the same vein.

Let's look at the neutrals. Those neutrals… is there a way you can amp up the value alignment? Getting the groceries is pretty value neutral for me, but if my husband and I trade off doing it, it means that one of us gets a little alone time which is definitely a value we both hold (love those kids, but breaks are needed). That way when it's my turn to get the groceries, there's an added pep in my step and an Americano in my hand.

And finally, the check marks. Go back over them and add a star next to the activities that light you up. The ones that just make you happy, engaged and thriving. Perhaps there aren't many, that's okay, but do them FIRST. Prioritize them. Those are your zones of genius, the things you are best at and enjoy doing, even if they don't make you any income. Remember we talked about hobbies? Make time for them each week. Fifteen minutes of joy goes a long way.

The balance of minutes and hours isn't important. At the end of the day it's how these activities make you feel. I want you to honor the yeses in your life, the time spent in alignment with what you value. Make the time, don't feel guilty about that time, and prioritize it. I want to see some "heck yes" moments on that calendar more often than not.

We've spent the bulk of this chapter talking about how to create those boundaries to say no. If you're doing an activity kicking and screaming, that's not great. There has to be a way to alter, tweak or reassess how you do it so that you're not completely going against the grain of your values. Is there a cost to a no? Sure. In many cases saying no has an impact. You don't want to disappoint other people, but are you disappointing yourself and your own goals in the process? We are part of a broader community, but aim for things to be mutually beneficial.

Say you're asked to volunteer for something and you're just not interested. Is there a way to support the organization or cause that is more in alignment with what matters to you or your area of expertise? Probably. Or can you refer them to someone who is a better fit? Do it. Your time matters.

This calendar audit can feel hard the first few times you do it, but rip off the band-aid and what you're actually doing is creating time and energy in your own life.

Recap

- Boundaries are critical to protecting yourself, your energy and your values.
- Boundary management is rooted in knowing your values, defining a clear boundary including an outcome, communicating it (where applicable), and reinforcing it. Simple, but not always easy.
- We can often step over our own boundaries, so start small by protecting your time and auditing your calendar.

Don't forget to head to stresslessin90days.ca for this week's journal reflections and action items.

WEEK FOUR
HABITS THAT SERVE YOU

According to brain scans, we make an average of 35,000 decisions in a day. Holy smokes, right? We decide what we are going to eat in a day, and how to manage each email, notification or phone call. We decide what we are going to wear, how to motivate our kids (or pets!), and when we're going to fit in that random errand. We make hundreds of decisions on the drive to work, scanning for pedestrians, choosing to gun that yellow light or whether to take another route to save two minutes. Thousands of micro-decisions go through our mind on the daily and our decisions lead to the actions we take.

Researchers believe that between 50-90% of our decisions and actions are habitual, we do them without thinking. Conservatively, **half of your actions come down to your habits.** Half of your actions and decisions are made unconsciously. A habit is a settled or regular tendency or practice, and can sometimes be difficult to change without intention.

Now that you know where you're going (your deep down why), what you value (getting in alignment with your guiding principles) and you have the boundaries to make space for your needs, this is where we can focus on building the habits to support lasting stress management.

Stress is a Habit

What do habits and stress have to do with one another? Be it traffic, a certain coworker emailing you or your in-laws - we tend to respond to stress the same way MOST of the time. How you choose to respond in times of stress is a habit. Do you reach for comfort food, a drink, a smoke, or vent to a friend? Does your blood start to boil when you disagree with someone, or do you tend to go down the rabbit hole of negative self-talk?

Our stressors (the external and internal situations that lead to us feeling stressed) are not going anywhere. You still have to drive in traffic, deal with your co-worker, experience loss, and have difficult conversations. The only thing you can control is your response, which we now know is habitual.

We can build proactive habits that serve to decrease our stress over time or we can lean on easy habits that are comforting in the short term but damaging to our stress levels in the long run. If you can begin to shift your habits from damaging to supportive, over time you'll find that you have less stress and more joy and energy.

But how did you wind up with the habits you currently have?

Your Environment Shaped Your Current Habits

Throughout our lives we gain new habits and shed old ones. Initially influenced by the people we grew up with, these habits include how we communicate, how we handle pressure, traditions, our work ethic and so on. This is not to say you're a carbon copy of your parents. As a child you reacted to how your parents engaged with you. You learned habits of how your household ran, how to respond to conflict, and how to communicate with others. On the flip side, parents often think that they are treating you exactly as they were treated. How often is that actually the case? Your parents grew up in a different era with different societal norms, and so naturally treated you differently whether consciously or not. Some habits will carry over generation to generation and some will shift with the times and new dynamics.

Your youth is such an influential time in your habit development. We mirror what we see, so if you had a parent who was prone to quick temper and yelling, you may find that is your go-to reaction whether you like it or not. If you grew up feeling unsafe in your household, the habit of staying quiet and small could be deeply ingrained by the time you leave the nest. You may have grown up with role models who reinforced that anything was possible, encouraged creativity and imagination, and as a result you take more risks and make bold choices.

Each new environment you integrate with also influences your habits. Your college roommates liked to party and so you ended up partying frequently. Your co-workers gossip and you find yourself doing the same. Your team members are always working overtime and so you start burning the midnight oil. We are incredibly influenced by our environment, most notably the people we spend the most time with.

So, how do our family of origin, the people we spend the most time with and our environments influence our habits? Habits are developed in our brains over time. Donald Hebb said "Neurons that fire together, wire together," meaning **the more you do something repeatedly, the stronger you're making the neural pathways in your head.** A strong neural pathway means this becomes your new normal response. And so, if you grew up in a household of germaphobes or yellers, over-sharers or emotional eaters, in all likelihood you've developed strong neural pathways that reinforce those habits.

You might be thinking about how you are the opposite of your family, roommates and coworkers in so many ways, and that very well may be true. What likely happened is that the way they behave and the things they value are out of alignment with your own, so you consciously make decisions and build habits that support your own values.

The beauty of neural plasticity is that our brains have the ability to change over time. You CAN rewire a habit. It takes time and energy, but it can be done.

How to Rewire Habits

So, how do you rewire hardened habits? First, you have to shine a spotlight on them.

At one point during writing this book, we were in the early weeks of COVID-19. Our family of four had been in close quarters for six weeks, and we all know this magnifies every challenge. One day my husband and I had a sit down. I was unbelievably annoyed that he kept forgetting to turn the dishwasher on at night. In a righteous way I laid out all the ways he could make this habit more obvious and create cues to ensure it is turned on at night and I'm not greeted with sticky dishes in the morning.

His response?

Yes, he could do that. But could I also please stop dumping my purse wherever I pleased.

I was taken aback for a second, because I wasn't conscious of dumping it on the floor. Yet, over that next week, I started to realize he was right. Monday it was left by the dreaded dishwasher, Tuesday on the couch, Wednesday by my shoes, Thursday by the TV. Each day I'd notice it and hang it where it belonged, but isn't it funny how this habit had gone unnoticed by me for so long?

It will be the same for you. Sometimes we know when we have 'bad' habits. We know that when we're bored or lonely, we go to the chips (or at least I do). We know that when we're stressed, we might reach for the glass of wine. We know that we dread getting up in the morning and so the snooze button is our best friend.

But what about all the habits under the surface that contribute to our stress, our health and our happiness? How do they work?

The Habit Cycle

A negative email sends you spiraling. The smell of a cinnamon bun makes you salivate. The journal on your bedside table reminds you to write down your gratitude list for the day. Your calendar on the fridge keeps you on track for the day's activities. Everything I just described? They are the cue in a habit cycle.

The best book out there on habits is *Atomic Habits* by James Clear. He makes the concept of habits so tangible that you can immediately apply the skills in your everyday life.

Based on his book, let's talk about the habit cycle. Every habit is made up of a cue, a craving, a response and a reward. The cue is what triggers a desired change in state. For me, every time I drive by Starbucks, whether I'm caffeinated or not there is a slight craving that arises. Or when the notification of a text pings, I'm tempted to grab my phone. These are all cues.

The craving is a desired change of state. You might genuinely be craving a specific food or drink, or perhaps you're craving a relief from boredom, comfort, connection, laughter, escape... After a hard day of work, how many of us end up on the couch watching TV? I'll put my hands up! And how often do we say "I just want to zone out"? That zoning out is what we're craving, the TV is simply the vehicle for us to stop thinking about our day.

The response is the behavior you choose to take to meet that craving. Do you eat the cookie? Do you work out? Do you walk away from the hard conversation?

And finally, the reward is whether or not you satisfied that craving. Not all rewards are created equal. I come from a family of emotional eaters. Feeling stressed - food is the comforting go-to response, but more often than not the reward is short-lived. Yes, eating the box of Girl Guide cookies is deeply satisfying for five minutes, but beyond that I find it doesn't quell the feelings, and so the cycle repeats itself.

Alternatively, certain rewards are longer lasting. These tend to be the best rewards, and they usually align with behaviors that serve us. During the first few weeks of COVID-19, my heart would race out of my chest. A few times I actually worried I was going to have a panic attack or even a heart attack. In previous times I would have resorted ONLY to food as the coping mechanism. Don't get me wrong, I most definitely indulged in some quarantine baking (a failed pavlova to prove it!), but I made a habit of choosing exercise, fresh air and sunshine as my frequent response.

When you raise your heart rate through movement, you're signaling your brain to trigger the parasympathetic nervous system. A fifteen-minute walk or workout would help me feel calm and refocused for a few hours. A much longer lasting reward than the cookies.

Another note on the reward - it may not be satisfying in the moment, but the outcome matters as well. Doing my taxes is not fun for me, but getting the tax refund on the other end is. Scrubbing my shower is not joyful, but seeing less grime is...well not joyful, but satisfying.

So now that you know how a habit cycle works, what are those stress-related cues? You cannot change the cue. That co-worker will still irritate you. The car will still cut you off in traffic. It will rain when mother nature wants to rain. The only thing you have control over is your response.

Bearing that in mind, what are the new responses that you can try that will give you a similar reward? Remember, the reward is how satisfied you are with meeting a change in your desired state.

Yes, if you're stressed a gin and tonic could work… temporarily. Or a bar of chocolate hits the spot… for a little while. Alternatively, things that could work when you're stressed are journaling, walking outside, sitting on your porch stoop and feeling the sunshine on your closed eyelids, a hot shower, doing an art project, talking to a friend or partner, etc. You need to create a go-to list of coping mechanisms that work FOR YOU. Refer to it often. In those early days of changing your behavior, it's going to feel new and maybe even uncomfortable.

People want things to be comfortable and easy. We rarely like feeling uncomfortable, unless we know there is a meaningful reward at the end.

So, how many days does it take to create a habit? Say it out loud. Twenty-one! Thirty! Sixty! Ninety! I can hear your brain ticking through all the articles you've read that promised "x days to create a habit." Well, if you don't have certain principles in place, it may never stick.

James Clear talks about four key principles that need to be in place in order to create a new habit. It must be obvious, easy, attractive and satisfying. If you think back to all the habits you've tried to build that didn't last, ask yourself if you covered all four of these bases? If you're wanting to create a new habit of filling in a gratitude journal before bed, is the journal in an obvious place? Have you made it easy by keeping the practice short and sweet? Is it attractive to you and do you find some joy in the process? Are you satisfied with how it makes you feel? Keep this in mind as you develop new habits.

What if you want to break a habit? According to Clear, you flip the principles. Make it invisible, difficult, unattractive, and dissatisfying. Making something obvious or invisible comes down to the cue. Remember we said you can't get rid of the cue? It's still true, you can't, but you can proactively work to make it a bigger part of your environment or to take it out entirely. I told you I have a love for Starbucks that runs deep, but if I were to change my commute and not pass that glorious mermaid sign in the sky, I'm less likely to have the cue triggered.

Tying It Back to Your Stress

Now you know the basics of the habit cycle and what needs to be in place to create a lasting habit, but how does that tie into stress? I want you to actively think about all the cues that trigger stress in your life. Make that list of every stress trigger, large or small.

From there I want you to outline the habit cycle. What is the desired change in state you're craving? What is your usual go-to response and does it feel like a lasting reward? If it's adding to your stress over time, that's not very rewarding.

Once you have this information, you're equipped with the awareness to start making changes. What response will give you a similar reward for a longer period of time? Truth time - if this is an ingrained habit, you may need to try out responses that you've never tried before. I remember in my burnt-out corporate days when a coworker talked about how going to the gym just made her feel so energetic *hair toss*. I wanted to punch the gal as I sat there, tomato-faced from my efforts on the treadmill. Years later, moving my body DOES give me energy, but it took time and it's only one of my coping mechanisms for stress.

So, make that list and start trying out new responses. Try them more than once, because the first time is often uncomfortable or we're focused so much on the effort and the trying of the new thing that we don't get a chance to experience the benefit. We're too distracted to be in the moment.

Real life example - as I write this chapter in the past week I've received three emails that felt like major let downs. Nobody was mean or cruel to me, but I'd lost out on opportunities and was passed over for other people. I cried, felt angry, useless and impostor syndrome was in full effect. Usually I'd turn to food, but on these particular days I was really flexing that resilience muscle. So, what did I do? I sat with the mother-trucking-feelings. And it sucked. Big time. I sat in the sad feelings, I cried, I released, and after ten to thirty minutes (depending on the specific day and email) I was able to come out of that sadness fog, name what I was feeling and recognize the mistruths running through my head.

I'm not useless. I'm not a failure. My business isn't doomed. Those people aren't necessarily better than me. Perhaps you've had moments like this too. Once I processed the sadness, I was able to re-frame and recognize that those opportunities weren't meant for me. I started to look at what the successful candidates were doing differently and what I could learn from them. I was also able to zone in on what sets me apart and leverage that for future opportunities. As far as the habit cycle goes – it was a choice of short-term discomfort (sitting with the feelings) for a longer lasting reward (processed feelings and understanding for the win).

My friend and business coach, Stephanie Pollock, often talks about "the messy middle" where things are hard and uncertain before they get better. Sometimes we're in the messy middle for a while, and sometimes we can move through it, moment to moment. But we don't get through to the other side - ever - without the mess.

In those moments we need to find new responses to get to a better reward. And you do it one day at a friggin time. Don't try and rewire all your habits at once. That would be setting yourself up for failure and we don't have time for that.

Start small. Sometimes even the idea of trying something new for one week feels overwhelming. Focus on today. You're much more likely to achieve the one-day goal, and then when you wake up the next day, you'll have the success of Day One behind you which fires up your dopamine response and encourages you to keep going.

For my fellow friends who like to only start things if they know they can finish them - first off, I hear you. Secondly… that means you're making the task too large. I hear people say that if they can't spring clean the entire house or an entire room then what's the point.

Well, let me tell you, whether you're busy because of your workload, family and friend commitments or a combination thereof, we're not all flush with free time. Instead get into the habit of a little bit at a time, but give it firm parameters so that you feel like you did complete something start to finish.

If you've seen the Marie Kondo series *Tidying Up* you know that it can seem overwhelming to completely organize your house. Kondo's method has you go category by category (clothing, papers, sentimental, etc.) and it can make a big mess in the short run as many people can attest to. What she does is break it down into clear steps for you. But if that is still too overwhelming, go micro. Pick one and only one drawer to organize.

What's your habit equivalent of that one drawer? Five minutes to delete as many emails as possible? Folding and putting away one basket of laundry instead of three? Weeding one section of your garden? Simply setting a timer can help in building that habit of starting and finishing based not on the outcome, but on the time you've allotted yourself.

Proactive Habits

You've outlined the triggers for your stress and what your new response will be. Now how can you proactively avoid or minimize those triggers in the first place? What are the habits that you can begin to build so that you're feeling mentally, emotionally or physically more resilient so that these stress triggers don't bowl you over?

These are some of the proactive habits my clients have developed:

- "Waking up before my kids so I can drink coffee or do something for myself in peace before I'm responsible for anyone else."
- "Taking thirty minutes twice a week for hobbies that fuel me – right now it's building LEGO!"
- "Saving my favorite book for bedtime so I'm motivated to get into bed and be screen-free."
- "Writing in my journal at the end of the workday to download any stress before I go home."
- "I work from home, so I save my favorite playlist for the end of the workday and have a dance party. It helps me transition into "home mode" and leave work at my desk."

The habit I want you to work on regardless of your specific goals is the habit of showing up. Whether it's five minutes a day or an hour, the act of showing up for yourself and your goals is powerful. You won't feel like you want to do it each day, but five minutes is better than nothing. Nora Roberts, famed romance and mystery author, is well known for writing hundreds of novels. Is she inspired every day? Hell no. When asked how she writes even on hard days, she said, "The muse is a fickle bitch." It's about showing up each day and making THAT the habit instead of the outcome. The outcome will materialize if you show up persistently.

. . .

To access the workbook and dissect your habits go to stresslessin90days.ca.

Quick Goal Check In

This is the point in my work with one-to-one and group clients where I check in on the goals you've set for your ninety days. Have they shifted a little? Is something else rising to the surface as being more important? That's okay! This is where we begin to crystallize what truly matters for you and where the juiciest progress can be made.

Often, we have multiple things we'd love to achieve at once. Literally as I write this book I want to excel at work, write an awesome book, have a smooth transition to our new life in British Columbia... and oh yeah, I'd love to be taking care of my physical and mental health at the same time. It's incredibly difficult for us to tackle multiple goals simultaneously. It's not impossible, but usually you need to see a bit of progress in one area, to build some sustainable habits, and then you can begin to refocus some energy to a different goal while the other one ticks along. Think of it like the various pots on the stove while you're cooking a big meal. You put effort into one, you simmer it, then you start the next. You can't create three dishes all at once.

So, what in particular is coming up for you as being your juiciest goal? If you think about the next sixty days, if you only achieved one of those goals, which is most important for you?

That one. Prioritize *that* one.

Recap

- Half of our daily actions are habitual and unconscious. Start to bring awareness to the habits that aren't serving you and switch those up first.

- Create a list of new responses that will satisfy the craving you're seeking in a more constructive way.
- Ensure that new habits meet the principles of being obvious, easy, attractive and satisfying.
- Start small to see bigger gains. Break projects down into micro chunks.
- Create the habit of showing up for your goals each and every day. The amount of time doesn't matter.

WEEK FIVE

SELF-SABOTAGE

"I JUST DON'T HAVE ENOUGH WILLPOWER."

We've been trained to believe that some people are born with a huge amount of willpower while others have none. Hopefully after reading the last chapter you now have the awareness that it's not really about willpower, it's about how well you set up your habits to satisfy your cravings.

We're now in week five which is when the wheels can begin to fall off for many people. We're pretty good at doing something consistently for three to four weeks. Motivation and energy can carry us through a month. Week five is often when the proverbial hits the fan and our goals are tested. Why? Because it's when self-sabotage starts to creep in, if it hasn't already.

What is self-sabotage? **Self-sabotage is when we are consciously or unconsciously taking steps to inhibit our happiness or future success.**

Now, logically, you read that definition and you might be thinking… *Why would I want to harm my happiness or success? I mean, that sounds like it goes against everything I want, right?* At the end of the day, we all want to be happy and to be successful, so why would we sabotage that?

There are so many good reasons that we self-sabotage. I say *good* reasons, because whatever the reason or reasons are, they are compelling enough for you to get in your own way. The first step is understanding why you're doing what you're doing.

Reason #1: We Fear Failure

This is so common. We want other people to perceive us as successful and not as failures. So, if you're about to take on a habit change or a new life direction, that comes laden with uncertainty. You can't know the outcome, which means you don't know that success is guaranteed.

What if I fail? What if I embarrass myself? What if I end off worse than I was to begin with? 'What if's' swirl and make us doubt ourselves. The unknown often leads to us not even giving it a try. Even though you might be disappointed by not trying, at least you know for sure what the outcome will be. No trying equals no change. Clear as day.

There is no such thing as certainty. Not in relationships, not in jobs, not in the consistency of our beliefs. Nothing is certain. So, if you're someone who struggles with the fear of failure, I want you to grab a post-it note and a pen, then write down "nothing is certain" and place it somewhere prominent to constantly remind yourself of this truth.

We need to rewire how you think about failure.

Let's also talk about the word failure. Not long ago I was asked in a job interview what failures I've had in my career. To be honest, I felt a little stumped. Not because something has never gone off course or 'wrong', but because failure implies a lack of a successful outcome. The question is then, how do you define success? If I have learned from an experience, pivoted along the way or decided that it's no longer a strategic fit, then I don't consider it a failure. It served a purpose.

Connotation is so incredibly important. Things have not gone as planned, for sure. Things have been hard, stressful and an uphill battle, but if I found a new outcome, it wasn't a failure.

So, ask yourself, how are you defining failure? And could you maybe try shifting your perspective so that what matters is growth, change, or deciding something isn't a fit?

You may have heard the story of Sara Blakely, the inventor of Spanx. Growing up, each night at the dinner table her father would ask all the kids, "What did you fail at today?" He was genuinely interested, because failing meant they had pushed themselves out of their comfort zone and tried something that wasn't a slam dunk. Failure was good. Imagine if you grew up with that mentality. How would your life be different?

You can't re-do your childhood, but you *can* start to rewire your brain. Failure is good. Failure is growth. Like I said before: **it's not a failure if you're growing or pivoting**. Decide which version of failure resonates for you, then remind yourself of it every single damn day. Catch yourself when you have feelings of failure and immediately state your new definition. You have years of neural wiring to undo, but it can be done, one reinforcement at a time.

Reason #2: We Fear Success

Wait, what? Why would we fear success? Well, again, success comes with change. If I get that dream job, will people think I'm making too much money? Will I start to have less free time? Will I be stressed out? Will I become someone I don't recognize?

We make a laundry list of conjectures about what success in one area of our lives could do to another, so much so that we can talk ourselves out of an opportunity.

In her book *Lean In*, Sheryl Sandberg shared how common it was for young women to fear taking a promotion because they wanted to be mothers, even though many of them weren't pregnant or in a relationship. The idea of a promotion made them second guess the impact of that success on their personal life before those factors were even a reality. This is self-sabotage in action.

I have often wondered what my life would look like if my business went stratospheric. I wonder about the impact on my family, so I ask myself questions like "Would I have as much time for them?" or, "Would I face a ton of online backlash?" etc. When I notice I'm getting in my head about what ifs, I remind myself that I can only control myself, the work that I put in each day and how I show up for my family. I'm not all-knowing, nor do I turn all the levers. Getting in my head only stops me from enjoying and thriving today and it's the same for you.

Some of the best advice I ever received was that we don't have a decision to make *until we have a decision to make*. Let that one sink in. Stop talking yourself in circles about all the possible outcomes until you have a choice to make. Don't spiral with potential obstacles until you're offered the job, get the opportunity or need to make the call on what's next. You'll save yourself time, energy, and a heck of a lot of stress. Focus on what's immediately in front of you. You don't have a decision to make until you have a decision to make.

Reason #3: We Want Control

Given I was just talking about focusing on what I can control, I'd like to give a shout out to all my control-loving friends out there. I literally just micromanaged my husband an hour ago, then had a moment of self-awareness and said to him "I hate micromanagers, but I just told you how you should wash those bell peppers, didn't I?" He smiled, shook his head and sarcastically said "No…" We both know I like control.

If you fall into this category, a lot of things can stress you out, as well as cause you to self-sabotage. If you want control, you're going to lean into the decisions or actions where you know the outcome. The challenge is that we cannot know for sure how many things will turn out.

In the summer of 2020, my family and I were road tripping down to Waterton Lakes in Southern Alberta. It is spectacular down there. The views are stunning, the lake is brisk, and the poor cell service means I switch off. That is, until we drove over a microscopic nail and ended up at a gas station in a small town with two kids in the back during COVID-19 as the air hissed violently from our tire.

We called our motor association for a tire change (we only had an emergency tire), but were told that due to the pandemic if our car needed towing we weren't allowed to be in the car with roadside assistance. I pictured walking along a country road in 29 degrees Celsius with a stroller and a toddler. I won't lie, I cried a bit. Okay, a lot. All my plans felt like they were going to shit and it all felt out of my control.

In the end, we got the spare tire on, drove super slowly to Waterton given the speed limitations of an emergency tire, had our puncture repaired at a bicycle shop and all was well with the world. But in the moment? It felt intense. And, this is pretty much how anything I cannot control goes. In the moment it feels big, and with even just a little hindsight I realize the worst-case scenario is rarely the worst case and there are workarounds. Is it inconvenient and off script? Sure. End of the world? Rarely.

If you tend to go to worst-case scenarios, what you're experiencing is called catastrophic thinking. In order to combat catastrophic thinking, first you have to verbalize what is happening. "Hello, Victoria, you are catastrophic thinking here!" Next you need to say to yourself, "Okay, I've figured out the worst-case scenario, but what is the best-case scenario? What good could actually come from this situation? How could it all be okay in the end?" Then you have to realistically assess which is more likely to happen based on facts and evidence. Was I likely to be walking by the side of the road for miles back to my hometown? No. Somebody in my life would have come to pick me up, regardless of COVID, because we don't leave each other stranded. Deep breaths.

If you are striving towards a goal or a vision for your life, things will go off course regardless of how well you show up. You need to prime yourself for those hard times and tell yourself "Here is what I will do in those moments…", or that, in the words of Marie Forleo, "Everything is figureoutable." You have to get out of your own way first.

Reason #4: We Want Acceptance

One of the biggest regrets that people have on their deathbed is that they didn't fully embrace who they were and what they loved to do sooner. This starts young. I bet if you look back on photos of yourself from your school days there were a whole lot of fashion trends that didn't age well, you maybe didn't speak up as often as you wish you would have, or you did activities that weren't really *you*.

You were trying to be accepted by the crowd. I remember it vividly. In grade four or five, I participated in the school talent show with a little dance. I was put on stage with two other girls (popular girls) and we each got ninety seconds of our song to dance to.

Later that evening, a group of five popular girls showed up at my home on their bicycles, and they came in to give me a makeover. I *so badly* wanted to fit in and feel like one of the pretty girls. But that little spell of popularity came and went in a flash and I feel like, for most of my school days, I kept chasing the feeling of being cool and accepted. I was decidedly not cool by the 'popular' standards, which in retrospect weren't so cool either.

Human beings are pack animals. From a survival standpoint, it's wired into our DNA that if we're excluded from the tribe, we might not live for very long. But in modern times, being alone is unlikely to lead to a life or death situation.

We don't only do this in school. There are unwritten rules at work, in public settings, on social media. There are norms that society at large says are acceptable for women versus men, and it's up to us to buck those norms to live in alignment with what we believe in.

Alexandria Ocasio-Cortez could have just let it slide when she was called a "fucking bitch" by Congressman Yoho, but she took a stand about what is and is not acceptable behavior. Women around the world know what it is like to be called a bitch in the workplace, and many of us have self-sabotaged and not stood up for ourselves because we don't want to rock the boat. Well, sometimes the boat is not worth the passage. We can build our own damn boat.

You have to ask yourself" **this acceptance that you desire, is it worth it?** Are the people granting acceptance worthy of your time, energy, and stress? Is it worth being out of alignment with your values? I can't answer that for you, and your answers may change over time, but it's important that you take the time to assess it.

Reason #5: We Don't Feel Deserving

I'm not experienced enough for that job. I'm not attractive enough to ask that person out. I'm not a good enough parent. I'm not smart enough to make that decision. I'm not [fill in the blank] enough.

I've yet to meet a person who didn't have some area of their life where they had some insecurity around their worthiness. Somehow, at some point, you received this message, either implicitly or explicitly. You internalized it, played the message on repeat, and here we are today. You may present confidence to the world and feel like an imposter on the inside.

But is it true? Is it true you're not deserving of [insert the blank]? Says who? Why? So what if there are other people ahead of you on whatever curve you're measuring yourself against. They're not you. You're not them. They don't live your unique life and experiences, nor you theirs. If you don't give yourself the opportunity to even try, you'll never allow yourself to be deserving either. You cut yourself off at the feet.

No matter what, you are always deserving of love and respect. Start with some self-love and self-respect and you'll go a long way.

Reason #6: We Play the Blame Game

If it weren't for *this* person, I'd be more successful. If it weren't for *that* experience, I'd be fine. It's all the same. It's about one thing between you and your desire. I hear statements like this a lot. I've *made* statements like this a lot.

You don't have control over anybody else. You only have control over your actions, thoughts, and how you care for yourself. That's it, and yet that's incredibly powerful.

You're not reading the tea leaves. If that person weren't so challenging, maybe you would be more successful, but maybe not. Maybe it's actually the mindset that you've got that is holding you back and not that other person. It's not always the case, but sometimes it is. There are no absolutes. Maybe it's not that you don't have a college degree, but that you aren't showing interest in taking on new projects (perhaps because you doubt yourself...).

Let me be clear, I'm not suggesting you turn this around and blame yourself for everything — that's not it at all. It's about seeing what opportunities and potential are available to you that you can be empowered to take charge of.

When you get into the blame game, you do it for good reasons. Your mind wants to preserve the image it has of you. Psychologically, you want to protect yourself from accountability. But that's all about keeping you safe and comfortable, and by this point you know that comfort and growth are not congruous. We need to get uncomfortable to achieve our goals.

Reason #7: We Like the Known

Similar but different to wanting control, psychologically we feel comfort in knowing what to expect. Very few people actually thrive off of the new, unanticipated, thrown-at-you challenges as a way to consistently live their lives. The majority of us like to know what to expect.

But we can't always know.

What we *can* do is create systems and routines that bolster the familiar *known* feeling we crave when we can while giving ourselves room for the uncomfortable unknown at other times.

This list could be longer, but these seven reasons sum up why most people self-sabotage. And they *are* good reasons. Our brains and our bodies were developed with survival in mind, and psychologically, many of your goals and dreams feel counter to survival… even if you and I both know that's not logical. We have to work against that biological wiring.

Dr. Kirk Honda is a psychologist based in Seattle with the appropriately named *Psychologists in Seattle* YouTube Channel. He does a great series where he reacts to pop culture and describes what he sees happening in his professional opinion.

If you were as addicted to *Love Is Blind* as I was, you already know it's an experiment on whether or not you can fall in love without seeing the other person. Part of what made it binge-worthy was how the couples communicated with one another.

One of the couples (you know which one if you were a viewer!) faced a ten-year age gap. The man was ten years younger than the woman he became engaged to, and he repeatedly said that it didn't bother him, because what mattered was the connection. The woman seemingly was a great fit for this man (granted viewers only see the highlight reel producers chose to show), but she kept bringing up the age difference again and again.

Dr. Honda did a reaction video to this series, and I'll never forget him saying, "Our efforts to protect ourselves from rejection and pain often end up causing rejection and pain." Think about that again — our efforts to protect ourselves from rejection and pain often end up causing rejection and pain. You likely have a few examples of this in your own life. You fear being dumped, so you break up with the person first. You worry you'll fail if you apply for a new job, so you stay stuck in your current role. You're basically ensuring a dissatisfying outcome in the effort to protect yourself. So, what do we do about it?

Thank Your Self-Sabotage

Thank it? Why would I thank the part of me that is getting in the way of my happiness and success? Because it was doing it for a damn good reason. I want you to go a little woo woo here and now that you know why you self-sabotage, I want you to get a scrap of paper and write out a little thank you note. Thank it, recognize the good reason it existed and the purpose it served to your life, and let it go. It can look a little something like this:

> *Thank you, self-sabotage. You were trying to keep me from getting hurt. I appreciate you wanting to keep me safe, but I no longer need you. I'm strong enough to try a different way.*

This names what is going on and it allows you to release it. Now, take each slip of paper that you came up with and actually let it go. Burn it (safely!), flush it, rip it up, throw it in the garbage… whatever feels right for you, do that. Symbolism and ceremony are very powerful for us. In the Western world, we're seeing a decline in ceremony and traditions, and I actually think it's doing us more harm than good (I'm not specifically talking about religious ceremonies here). Ceremony or ritual allows us to psychologically process what's flying around our head, and I don't know about you, but my mind can be a hamster wheel, so it's refreshing to see a physical representation of what I'm processing.

So, burn that shit. Let it go. Only then can you actually make a change.

Identify Your Triggers

We talked about the habit cycle in the last chapter and it's going to be a useful tool for us throughout your ninety days. I want you to think back to all the times you've self-sabotaged. What are your triggers? What is the incident, be it a person, thought, event, etc., that initiates your behavior to self-sabotage? Make a list, because we tend to self-sabotage in more than one area of our lives.

One of my triggers is shopping. Like most people, body image has long been a challenge for me, and when I go shopping, I find I get easily frustrated if clothes don't fit or flatter as I'd anticipated. That can tend to make me feel upset, depressed, and feel like I just want to give up and eat a cookie.

NOW… *eating a cookie* is the behavior I took before I understood the trigger and the habit cycle. The trigger itself is shopping. Now that I know the trigger, I take tangible steps to change the behavior and get the reward I want — to buy clothes that make me feel good.

Next, I want you to ask yourself, what is it about those moments that actually upsets you? It's never the pair of jeans. I don't wish them harm! It's about how shopping tends to make me feel chubby, less than, and it sends me on a comparison spiral. Anybody else? What specifically about the situation triggers and upsets you?

Naming what you are feeling is super powerful, because it takes back ownership of the issue. I don't enjoy shopping, because shopping makes me feel bad about my body. Good, now I know what the trigger is and why it upsets me.

You have the ability to look at alternate behaviors to get the reward/outcome that you're aiming for. I shared the new behaviors that work for me before and during shopping.

Procrastination is a super common example of self-sabotage. We procrastinate for many different reasons. Some procrastinate because they feel overwhelmed, others because they feel like they thrive on limited time. Some struggle with decision fatigue and can't come to a clear choice, others put off the seemingly scary item on their to-do list while staying busy with less important tasks.

We procrastinate because it feels as though the longer we take to make a decision, the more likely we are to come to the 'right' decision. There is no such thing as the right decision. There just isn't. There's the best decision to be made with the information you have available. I could buy a house today, do all the 'right' things and get a home inspection and find out in two years it was a money pit due to unpredictable issues. Did I make a mistake? Or did I make the best decision with the information that was available to me at the time?

This is where your values come back in. When you make values-based decisions, you're making the best decisions for *you*, based on *your* criteria of what actually matters.

None of us are going out there actively trying to make terrible decisions. Some decisions take time, for sure. Sleeping on it is a real thing that allows you to take some emotion out of the process, because emotion can mask what's really going on. We've all had *that* relationship where we knew the person wasn't great for us, based on all the things we value, but at the end of the day, there was *something* about them.

Values-based decisions rarely fail you, because you can always look back and say in good faith that you acted in alignment with your values. So, when you're looking at alternative behaviors you can take to get the reward that you want, get out your list of values. Have them listed somewhere handy for the next 6-12 months until they are just part of how you live your daily life. Use that list as your criteria for which behaviors are the best next choice in your self-sabotage habit loop.

Got it?

I know it sounds easier than it actually is. In practice, you've got a lifetime of habits that may not serve you, so rewiring your brain is critical and we're going to deep dive that work next week.

1% Improvement

As James Clear discusses in *Atomic Habits*, what we're aiming for is not overnight transformation. We're looking at a one-percent improvement mentality. One-percent improvement each day creates incredible gains over time, just like compound interest. You'll get much further than someone who takes big leaps and then plateaus. You may not notice the change on a daily basis, but I promise that the slow, steady consistency is what will change the game.

This is a meaty topic and important to process, so make sure you dedicate time to the questions in the workbook which you can find at stresslessin90days.ca.

Recap

- Identify the good reason that you self-sabotage, thank it, and ceremonially let it go.
- You don't have a decision to make until you have a decision to make.
- It's never about *the thing*. Identify what your specific triggers are in moments of self-sabotage, then find a values-aligned behavior to try next time this comes up.

WEEK SIX

THE LIE OF CONTROL

HANDS UP IF YOU LIKE A CERTAIN AMOUNT OF CONTROL IN YOUR life. Perhaps you expect that if a meeting starts at ten, it actually starts at ten. Or maybe you have kids and just once it'd be nice if when you said "Get your shoes on, please" that they did it the first not the fifteenth time. You might get easily flustered when traffic delays your arrival at your destination, your flight gets cancelled or you run out of gas at an inopportune moment. Maybe you're preparing for a difficult conversation and it definitely doesn't turn out the way you had hoped. Or, you know, a global pandemic throws your routines, livelihood and sense of community out the window, for example.

We need control. We crave control. Control makes us feel safe and protected. Last week we dove into all the good reasons that you self-sabotaged. Did you notice how every single one had to do with control? We self-sabotage to control how we feel, how others treat us and/or to avoid uncertain outcomes. In order to protect ourselves from pain, we get in our own way because at least we feel we were in control of the outcome, even at our own expense. The need for control, whether it serves you or not, is powerful, so let's harness it in our favor.

Basics of Control

Maslow's Hierarchy of Needs is the principle that until our foundations are taken care of (food, water, shelter, safety), we can't focus on our higher needs (self-esteem or achieving our potential). So of course, if you're in a situation that challenges a basic need, you're going to feel out of control and stressed.

Have you ever tried applying for jobs when you're unemployed versus when you are employed but want to go elsewhere? It's a different energy you're bringing to your applications, isn't it? Without trying to, our applications while unemployed often have a hint of desperation to them, or we twist ourselves into shapes that we're not meant for because we need to pay the bills. Or perhaps we get the job offer, but we ask for less than we deserve, because we don't want to lose the opportunity altogether - at least that's what our lack of control makes us feel will happen if we ask for the salary that our experience deserves.

Being out of control is a feeling most of us try to avoid at all costs. If I make that to-do list, or buy that planner, or calendarize the crap out of my life, I'll be fine! Until you're not. Something hits you sideways and you stumble. How to regain control? It's not so much about regaining anything, as it is getting clarity on what you can and cannot control.

Alcoholics Anonymous is known for their regular use of the Serenity Prayer. "Grant me the serenity to accept the things I cannot change, the courage to change the things I can, and the wisdom to know the difference." Whether you're religious or not, these words are powerful. If you can live by them and not get sucked into the lie of control, you're on your way to a grounded life.

The Lie: I Can't Control Anything!

The biggest lie we tell ourselves when we're overwhelmed is that we can't control anything. I get it, I've said it. "Everything sucks. I can't control anything." We operate in this all or nothing state and our thinking spirals down. The question is: what are you trying to control, and could you ever really control it in the first place?

We cannot control anybody else. Not a dang person. I have toddlers, I've tried. As I write this chapter, my daughter is just about to turn three, and she currently wakes at 5:45 a.m. because of the chattering birds outside her window. "Go back to bed," I soothe and pat her back. "It's okay." She'll yawn, look at me, and simply say "No." At this point, she's had enough sleep, and no matter what I try, she's not having it. Whether it's a toddler, a romantic partner or a colleague, you cannot control their behavior.

Plenty of people I talk to say that they would rather be more easy-going or go with the flow, but that it's incredibly hard for them to do. They are juggling so many balls in the air and it can feel like you're the only one in charge of keeping them from dropping. Nora Roberts was asked how she juggled the needs of her work and her family. Note, it's rarely a question asked of men, but her answer was that "The key to juggling is to know that some balls you have in the air are made of plastic and others are made of glass."

The balls are going to drop. Sometimes it's because you yourself couldn't catch them because there were simply too many. Sometimes it's because you were tripped, someone bumped into you, or a gust of wind shifted the trajectory of that ball.

The first ball I want you to drop is the ball of trying to control the uncontrollable. So much frustration and dissatisfaction in life comes from people trying to control variables that are out of their reach, but not recognizing how much they *can* take ownership over.

The Difference Between What You Can and Cannot Control

Let's start with a short-list of what you cannot control:

- Your romantic partner, kids, friends, coworkers, family members, etc. Basically, anybody that isn't you
- Politics, political leaders, or the economy
- Your workplace
- Whether or not you're laid off or get that promotion

- The weather
- Who The Bachelor will pick (why do they always ignore MY pick for the winner?)

Try and control the above and you're on the fast track to stress.

What *can* you control? Many things. Many *important* things.

You can control your:

- Attitudes and mindset (I hear you scoffing already - wait until the end to hear me out!)
- Habits
- Self-care strategies
- Boundaries
- Language (to yourself and others)
- Preparation and worth ethic
- Space

Shifting Attitudes and Mindsets

Let's start with attitudes and mindset, because I bet you had a visceral reaction to that. *Victoria, this exact reaction proves that I cannot control how I react!* Well, good thing I didn't say you can control your reactions now isn't it?

From a psychological perspective, an attitude is a set of beliefs, emotions and behaviors towards a person, place, situation or thing. Attitudes are not set in stone. They're like clay, which we mold over time as we adapt and take shape from our life experiences. My attitude towards work used to be that it defined me. If I was failing it had a profound effect on me emotionally and physically. Nowadays, I have a much more balanced attitude towards work. Sure, sometimes it gets heightened, but I learned that I perform better when well rested, and most importantly that work is part of my identity, but it is not my entire identity. What attitudes do you have that have shifted over time?

Often our attitudes are built off of what we're told, what we experience, and how we choose to behave when something happens to us. If as a child you were reprimanded when you got things wrong, perhaps you now have the attitude where you don't try new things or avoid making a mistake at all costs. What attitudes do you currently hold at work, home and play? Which of them hold you back? Do these attitudes stop you from taking action, doing something you've always dreamed of, or getting yourself out of a negative situation?

Some common negative attitudes include:

- I can't…
- I'm not worthy of… or I don't deserve…
- I'm not [insert word] enough…
- This is how I've always done it…
- I'm the only one that can do…
- It's supposed to be hard
- I'm wired this way

I have a dear friend who would fight constantly with her ex. Cats and dogs. They'd have incredible make-up sex, but she was forever riding an emotional roller coaster. I'm sure at the time my relationship looked downright boring to her. My husband and I definitely bicker from time to time (mainly about household chores), but only once have we ever had a big blow out fight in ten years. When that same friend got into her current relationship, I remember her saying to me "I didn't realize it could be this easy." Her prior belief was that good relationships were not only worth fighting for, but required fighting.

How do you actively shift an attitude? It doesn't happen instantly. The first thing to ask yourself when you're struggling with an attitude that doesn't serve you is whether or not the attitude is true. Is it true that your partner couldn't possibly clean the house? Is it true that you can't take on a new task at work? Is it true that you're not worthy of respect? Is it true that this is the only way to do [task of your choice]? Hint: it's rarely true. There's an element of truth, otherwise you wouldn't believe it, but it's rarely the whole truth.

Once you assess that it's probably not true, the second thing to ask is what attitude could you adopt that would empower you? What mindset would help you to do the thing, be kind to yourself, have more faith in your abilities, etc.?

They can be minor but important language shifts. For example:

- I can't BECOMES I will figure out how
- I don't deserve BECOMES I am deserving of…
- I'm not [insert word] enough BECOMES I am enough
- This is how I've always done it BECOMES I can experiment with a different way
- It's supposed to be hard BECOMES It doesn't have to be this hard

Make the attitude and mindset shift on paper, then vocalize it. Say it again and again, day after day, until you believe it in your core.

Develop Habits That Serve You

How about your habits? In Week Four we outlined habit creation, and how to break habits that don't serve you. Remember, you cannot change the cue or the trigger. You will still get cut off in traffic. You could still get broken up with. The gossipy colleague could still pester you. You can, however, create habits to proactively manage stress, and to help you cope when stressful times happen.

During a very stressful period of my life when very little was in my control and days were long, I got into a habit of eating a snack around 8/8:30 p.m. while watching TV with my husband. Zero judgement if you are an evening snacker. The problem for me is that I was not hungry. Not even a little bit. And yet each night I turned to snacks to soothe the hard day. I don't like labelling things as good or bad. This wasn't a 'bad' activity, but it didn't serve my needs. As a result of the late snacking I slept poorly. And if I slept poorly, I woke up tired, then I got snappy, then the day felt longer, and you get the drill.

I decided to create a new habit where I didn't eat after six p.m. unless it's a special occasion. It's not about a diet, it's about good sleep. It's also about pushing myself to find new coping mechanisms, to sit with hard feelings, and to get better sleep. And so far, it has worked well for me. Beyond my children waking me in the night, I sleep pretty dang well.

If there is a stressor in your life right now what habit would help to manage it either proactively or reactively.

Back to the categories that you can control.

Intuitive Self-Care

Self-care looks different for everyone based on what fills them up emotionally, physically, mentally and spiritually. Some of these self-care activities will be daily or weekly habits that you build into your routine like sleep, movement, journaling, you-time, etc. Other self-care strategies might be less frequent or implemented on an ad-hoc basis. Perhaps you don't regularly see a counsellor, but you go when an intense situation arises. Intuitive self-care is about learning yourself inside and out, so that you can react with the right self-care strategy for your needs. Need rest? Take a nap! Overstimulated? Log off of social for the weekend, go for a walk without headphones, or take a much-needed vacation day off of work. Unmotivated? Try your hand at a new activity, do something creative or focus on a project (personal or professional) that always lights you up. The more you experiment, the more you can learn what works for you so that you can respond quickly in future.

Boundaries

Honestly, just go back to Week Three. If you haven't implemented the boundaries that you outlined as critical, why not? What's in your way? How can you break down the boundary to make it simple to deploy? Then layer on and layer on as you feel stronger and more courageous.

Language to Yourself and Others, Verbal or Physical

How we communicate is meaningful. Every time you tell yourself that you suck, you're not enough, you're not worthy, your brain quickly bounces that sent message back as information to decode. It looks for evidence that this is true. Yes, I did snap at my kids today, therefore I am a terrible mom, or so the lie goes.

We need to change this language. As we talked about earlier in your attitudes and mindset shifts, words matter. In the same way that you shifted your mindset in this chapter with a new choice of words, notice words that diminish or suppress you like: just, never, can't, shouldn't, I'm fine, it's no big deal (when it is), sorry (when you have nothing to be sorry for), etc. Even if the words don't escape your head, as they crop up, pause, snap them out of the air and replace them with the word or phrasing that supports your new mindset. If you repeatedly tell a child they are bad, they will believe it. If you repeatedly tell yourself you're not capable of a big challenge, you'll believe that too. Treat yourself with kindness and support in your language, and have a little faith.

When you're talking with others, it's also important to understand how they receive the words you're saying. I cringe when I say this now, but as a kid we threw around the word 'retarded' when we were trying to say that something was dumb or stupid. I was never intentionally trying to hurt someone with a disability, but I now know how hurtful a word like this is.

Microaggressions of language are when you use words or statements that either intentionally or unintentionally discriminate against a marginalized group. Be thoughtful and conscious of the language you use with others and how it can either uplift them, inform, or make them feel less than. And when you make mistakes, because you will (I do frequently), learn and do better. Know better, do better.

Work Ethic

If *The Great British Bake Off* is anything to go by, you can have the exact same ingredients and identical vague instructions for a technical challenge, and you can still get vastly different results. What makes the difference is your experience, preparation and work ethic. Do you simply show up and punch the clock at work, or are you invested in it, asking questions, learning and developing? When you need to have a difficult conversation with someone, are you winging it, or do you mentally rehearse it so you know you'll use the best words to get your point across? For the most part, you have control over how you prepare for a task, and the effort you put behind it. Howard Hendricks said, "You can control your choices, but you can't control the outcome of those choices."

Let's be clear – it's not about grinding yourself into the ground. We're not encouraging more burnout here. It's about releasing the tasks that don't move you forward, and focusing on the projects and activities that build traction towards your goals. Work smarter, not harder. What resources (human or otherwise) could help remove obstacles from your path? What piece of knowledge do you need to progress? Are there others who have forged the path you are aiming for, and what can you learn from their wins and their hiccups along the way? And remember, work ethic isn't only about how you perform in the workplace, but how you show up for yourself. You being at Week 6 shows work ethic, and that you've put in the effort to get here. Don't shortchange that. Acknowledge it, celebrate it, then use the tools to get to where you want to go.

Take Control of Your Space

Finally, there is a certain amount of control you have over your physical space, the interior of your car, your home, your workspace. Helen Youn is a Certified KonMari Consultant who I've had on the Girl Tries Life Podcast[1], and we had a great conversation about how our space and stress are connected. "When your environment is cluttered, it has the opposite effect [of sparking joy]. So, instead of supporting you to live your best life, it actually holds you back from doing what you want to do."

As Helen explained, our individual tolerance for clutter is different, because the objects and quantity of objects that spark joy for some, don't spark joy for others. I think of my almost eighty-year-old aunt who lives in the most gorgeous home in the English countryside. She has tons of beautiful objects that she's collected over a lifetime, and the living room is filled with piles of stacked books. She has artwork on every wall, couch cushions galore, textured wallpaper and it's hardly minimalist, but it sparks some serious joy. My aunt has an eye for colors, patterns and textures and weaves them together seamlessly.

You might want a minimalist, brand new space with perfect vacuum lines on the carpet, while another person wants their stuff visible. Make your space resonate with you and you'll feel aligned, more energetic and less stressed.

There are often limitations to what we can do with our space given budget, ownership, or perhaps because we're only in a space temporarily. That doesn't mean you can't make it feel more like you. It doesn't have to be expensive furniture or huge artwork. It can be in the details, in the scent of your space, some fake flowers because your dang cat would eat real ones, or your favorite pictures taped to the walls.

The spaces you occupy can lift you up or make you feel suffocated, so take some time to be intentional with them. And as someone who has recently moved to a smaller house and still has boxes to sort through and downsize, I'm here to tell you that one box, one surface, one drawer or one room at a time is more effective for your stress management than trying to do a little of everything all at once. Create a happy place for you, be it your desk or your bedroom, and keep that as a little sanctuary.

Where to Start? Connect the Dots.

My hope is that you're now realizing the many meaningful ways in which you can take control, but perhaps you're feeling a touch overwhelmed about where to start. There are so many options, right!

Let's get to it. Head to the workbook at stresslessin90days.ca, or simply grab a blank piece of paper and turn it landscape. Draw a line down the middle, and on the left side I want you to start writing down all the little and large things that are causing you stress or anxiety right now. Don't censor yourself. Take a few minutes and… go! It could look a little like this:

The things causing me stress are…	
• Too many meetings at work • Tight on rent this month • The news is depressing me • My teammate keeps emailing after hours • My partner isn't doing their fair share of chores	

Perfect, now on the right-hand side, I want you to write down all the things in your life that you can control, or begin to control right now. Take inspiration from the categories we've discussed in this chapter: attitudes, mindset, self-care strategies, boundaries, language, preparation and space. Go!

Mine looks a little like this:

The things causing me stress are...	The things I can control are
• Too many meetings at work • Tight on rent this month • The news is depressing me • My teammate keeps emailing after hours • My partner isn't doing their fair share of chores	• Blocking work time on my calendar • Delaying an unnecessary expense • Logging out of social media for a week • Going for a walk each day at lunch • Setting a firm boundary and internal out of office notice • Talking to my partner about my needs

Not only are you doing a bit of brain dump, but you're also giving evidence to your brain that what you're experiencing is valid. It's there, it's on paper, it's a real thing. Studies show that when we name what we're going through, there is less activity in our amygdala, which is where all our stress happens. So simply naming it is one step to stress less.

Now this is the fun part. I want you to start drawing lines from one side to the other from the thing that is stressing you out, to the thing that you can control that will help manage that stress. For example, if you're stressed out by the doom cycle of news, the thing you can control is deleting certain news or social media apps from your phone for a while, or curating your content consumption. Go!

The things causing me stress are...	The things I can control are
• Too many meetings at work →	• Blocking work time on my calendar
• Tight on rent this month →	• Delaying an unnecessary expense
• The news is depressing me →	• Logging out of social media for a week
→	• Going for a walk each day at lunch
• My teammate keeps emailing after hours →	• Setting a firm boundary and internal out of office notice
• My partner isn't doing their fair share of chores →	• Talking to my partner about my needs

Excellent! You may not have a line connecting each stressor to a strategy… yet. This is the homework you need to take away. I want you to take a little more time to think through what you could control that would help support your management of that stressor. There will be something - there always is.

Next, I want you to put a star on the two lines/connections that are most meaningful for you to work on this week. What can you begin to take control of so that you start stressing less as soon as possible? Make a plan for these action items, proactively remove or manage the obstacles, and then when you start to make traction and have the capacity to take on a new action item, do so.

This is an exercise that I regularly repeat in my own life. If things are starting to bubble up or feel like a lot, I write down what's stressing me out, what I can control, then make the connection. Seeing it all on paper makes it much more tangible to deal with rather than your monkey mind making you feel like you're being bashed around by the waves.

My final caveat – we talked about trying to control the uncontrollable, but I'd be irresponsible not to mention that there are times when we go too heavy into controlling what we can control. Think eating disorders like bulimia or anorexia. This is controlling what you eat or how you deal with it in a dangerous way. Same with working out to extreme measures.

Obsessive Compulsive Disorder (OCD) is an anxiety disorder where you have uncontrollable and intrusive thoughts, so as a result, people with OCD feel compelled to perform certain actions or behaviors. If you're suffering with any of the above, or frankly you feel like you're tipping into unhealthy behaviors around control, please seek professional support.

As the Serenity Prayer says, it's about the courage to know the difference between what we can and cannot control.

Recap

- You can't control everything, but you can control many impactful areas of your life. Be clear on the difference.
- Naming the stressors you're experiencing creates less stress in your brain - studies prove it. Name it to tame it.
- Connect the dots. When something is stressing you out, ask yourself what you can control that will help either proactively or reactively cope with the stress.

WEEK SEVEN

YOUR SPECIAL OCCASION IS NOW

ARE YOU #LIVINGYOURBESTLIFE? DOES YOUR DAILY LIFE LOOK LIKE a curated Instagram feed where each moment is manicured, joy-filled perfection like those influencers you follow? Of course it's not. And #neitheristheirs.

Joy isn't a constant state. Joy is about moments of happiness and elation. Nothing is permanent, especially not joy. Back to *Inside Out*, we don't function unless we have a myriad of emotions at play. You don't want sadness all the time, and you also don't want perma-joy, as appealing as it might sound.

Your life will be a roller coaster of good times and bad. Hard times hit us all, and while it's important to move through the pain and process it, it's equally important to know what brings you joy, so that you can create moments of it for yourself, even when it feels like the world is overwhelming you. You don't have to wait for a situation, a circumstance or another person to bring you joy, you can create it for yourself if you know the formula. Pockets of joy allow you to realign. They can spark energy where you've felt none, and they can bring you back to center, allowing you to put one foot in front of the other.

What Sparks Joy for YOU?

When I start with new clients and I ask them what brings them joy in their daily, weekly lives, I am usually met with a long pause…

…

…

…

It can get awkward.

If you can't think of five things this week that brought you joy, this is exactly what this chapter was made for.

First off, how do you define joy? Do you think it has to be a standout social media worthy moment? Because it sure as hell does not. For me, joy shows up in the tiniest of places. Joy is an iced americano on a hot day. Joy is my daughter giggling as I tickle her. Joy is a bite of caprese salad drizzled with balsamic reduction. It's also the big things like the vista on my favorite hike, or a day at the amusement park, or a walk on the beach. There is no standard for what joy is, because it's all about the little and large moments that make *you* smile.

In the Stress Less Habits Challenge that I began running in 2020, one month's challenge was about creating five minutes of pure joy a day. When I'd ask people on Instagram what brought them joy, I was flooded with examples, some that sounded like my worst nightmare (cleaning…) and others that I could totally get on board with (hello cheesecake!). What I also found was people consistently getting in touch to tell me how they suddenly realized how many things already brought them joy in their daily lives. They just hadn't been paying attention.

Now that certainly sounds familiar to my life. Isn't it funny how when we're glued to a phone or preoccupied with work that we don't notice the beauty around us? Joy is there, but sometimes we simply need to start paying more attention, and other times we need to put in a little bit of effort to create it from scratch.

But what if you're in the midst of a really trying time? When we're in a state of anxiety, depression or grief, it can feel incredibly hard to find and create joy, but in fact that's when you need it most and it is possible. It helps, however, to have your go-to list at the ready, which is what we'll develop this week.

Joy and Loss Can Coexist

When Jessica Janzen[1] was on a family holiday with her two-month old son, she couldn't have predicted how her life would turn on a dime. Seeking urgent medical attention, they found out that their son, Lewiston, had Spinal Muscular Atrophy (or SMA). The average child diagnosed with SMA has a life expectancy of 18 months, a crushing reality for any parent to face.

Jessica rallied with a fierce determination that no matter how many days, weeks or months her son had to live, she would bring as much joy to his life as possible. While confined to a hospital room, they would hold daily dance parties, play music, use an essential oil diffuser to make the room smell nice, dress up and do anything to make a clinical setting feel more joyful. They created countless smiles from their baby son.

When he passed away at one hundred and seventy-nine days old it was heartbreaking for their family, but they had begun on a journey to raise awareness of SMA, and have since raised hundreds of thousands of dollars to make the lives of SMA patients more comfortable and joyful while scientists search for a cure. Every year on Lewiston's birthday, the family holds an epic party to fundraise. It's not a pity party, as Jessica says, it's a celebration.

I also think of blogger, podcaster and influencer (among many roles), Linda Hoang. To follow her online is to feel a zest for life. From her bright outfits and colorful accessories, to her passion for the perfect egg yolk pop, to her intense love for animals and travel, Linda sparks major joy.

When Linda came on the Girl Tries Life Podcast[2] she shared her journey of unexplained infertility. For years she and her husband Mike had tried to naturally conceive a baby. They started young, so were quite surprised when things didn't happen as easily as we're often led to believe. How often do we talk openly about infertility?

Linda and her husband explored many options from artificial

insemination to IVF, and they've looked into adoption only for the agency they chose to shut down unexpectedly. Like millions of women who struggle with infertility, every month, when she gets her period it is yet another heartbreak.

And yet... Linda perseveres and looks for the joy. She doesn't ignore the pain. "Talking about it has helped," says Hoang. "A good cry can help you get on with your day." She has described the process she has been through in detail on her blog[3], and for her, sharing the experience has allowed her to normalize it and make others feel less alone, which in itself brings her joy.

Joelle Tomlinson is the bright face that brings you the morning news on CTV Calgary each weekday[4]. No matter what is going on in a news anchor's life, they need to present themselves in a professional, friendly manner. But sometimes the news hits a little close to home. In 2015, Joelle's brother Stefan died of a fentanyl overdose at 25 years old. "I see tragedies all the time. I write about them. I report on them. I anchor on them. But it had never happened to me. The moment it happens to you and you're on the other side, nothing can prepare you for that."

As a family, they made the decision to talk about what had happened to Stefan and bring awareness to the danger of fentanyl. Following the airing of the segment, Joelle received nearly a thousand messages from parents, or people who had been affected by a fentanyl overdose. The power of story helped families have conversations about mental health, grief, and made people feel less alone.

"When someone's life is cut short, you reflect it back on yourself." For Joelle, her brother didn't get to have so many experiences, so she now focuses on doing all the things she wants to in life. After he passed, Joelle traveled to Iceland to take part in a marathon that had been on her bucket list. She doesn't put off special moments for someday. She makes today that day.

This is just a sample of women I've spoken to on the podcast who have taken heartbreaking, often traumatic experiences and found a meaning going forward while looking for joy.

This isn't a "they can do it so you should be able to as well" kind of message. What I'm trying to demonstrate is that even in the hardest of times we can find and create moments of joy, but we have to be intentional about it. So how do we actively pull our attention, behavior and thoughts out of hard times long enough to grab onto joy? First, we have to rewire.

Notice-Shift-Rewire

A neuroscientist named Donald Hebb came up with a tool called Notice - Shift - Rewire. If you've ever heard the phrase "neurons that fire together, wire together," that's Donald Hebb. Essentially, each time you take a course of action, you're wiring your brain. That's why if your go-to coping mechanism (like mine has been) is emotional eating when you're upset, you can choose to actively rewire it in order to create new neural pathways so that a new normal is in your future.

The first step is **Notice**. You have to notice and bring awareness to what is going on. That's why we've taken the time to clearly identify your triggers. Notice when those negative thoughts are permeating your mindset. Next we need to **Shift** you out of that state. As Hebb says, one of the best ways to do that is to acknowledge a moment of gratitude. Find one little thing even if it's totally unrelated to the topic at hand that you are grateful for and sink into that feeling a little bit. Are you grateful for your family, your job, where you live, your warm coffee etc.? Take some deep breaths and let the gratitude trickle in.

That time that you took to soak it in, that 15-30 seconds? *That* was the **Rewiring**. You're wiring your brain for gratitude and a more positive outlook and training it out of a default negative state. Does it always work? Not always. Nothing is permanent, but the more you do this, the easier, faster and more efficient it will become.

Imagine those neural pathways in your brain are like an overgrown garden. You know you want to make a path to the fence, but right now it's so wild that you need to take a machete to it. It's hard work, you get super sweaty and you're exhausted. Next time, you're using a lawnmower. The following summer, you lay down some gravel. Eventually you can bound to the fence in five leaps and it's as though it was always that easy. This is what it's like to rewire those neural pathways.

If it feels too high stakes to try this when you're feeling really amped up, start practicing Notice-Shift-Rewire in low-stakes environments. When you're irritated at having picked the slow line at the grocery store, try it. Waiting in general is a great time to practice this. If you're stuck in traffic, try it. This starts to train your brain during a time that isn't as emotionally charged as others.

If I were to try Notice-Shift-Rewire for the first time when I was selling my house, it would have been incredibly hard to pull myself out of the emotional entanglement. Selling your house ranks as one of the top ten stressors we experience and now I understand why. So, if you can give yourself a solid grounding in this brain training on a daily basis, you're setting yourself up for success when the next painful stressors occur. You're stacking the odds in your favor.

Take an Audit of Your Joy

Let's start by understanding what brings and what kills your joy. We're going to look at four key categories: people, places, things and activities.

You can follow along in the workbook at stresslessin90days.ca.

People

Ask yourself who are the people that bring you joy? Who makes you smile or laugh so hard that your stomach hurts? Who makes you feel calm, peaceful, safe or loved? Who, when you spend time with them, makes you feel like the best version of yourself? Write down this list. It may not be a long list, and that's totally fine. This is about quality, not quantity.

Next you need to understand exactly what it is about these people that brings you joy? Get specific. My husband makes me laugh with his ridiculous jokes. My mom is the person that I can talk to about everything. My friend Amy, and co-creator of our group coaching program, is one of the people I can get vulnerable with quickly (as she often says, we don't do small talk). Different people fill different needs in our lives, and they can bring us joy for very different reasons.

Now flip it - who are the people that kill your joy? Often this list is easier. Isn't it funny how we let challenging people take up so much more of our brain space? Maybe this list is long, but also ask yourself how much time you generally spend with them. There are people who you'll engage with only a couple of times, so don't let their bad energy bring you down. Let's do something about those killjoys who for one reason or another you have to deal with regularly.

Now what about them kills your joy? We've all had that one coworker that can't help but gossip and complain. We all have that one extended family member that makes us feel like garbage. We have people in our lives who have caused us pain or trauma. What is it specifically about them that kills your joy? Usually it comes down to how they make you feel or an act of theirs that's caused you pain.

Now you've got your joyful versus your killjoy list. Ask yourself how you can spend more time with the people who fuel your joy and less with the people that suck the joy from your life?

Can you make a standing Zoom date (in person if you can!) with the dear friend you're currently only seeing once or twice a year? Can you set aside some intentional time each day with your partner or family members? I know for myself, with two young kids and the chores of day to day life, it's easy to just start existing with your partner. Yes, you watch Netflix together once the kids go to bed, but are you actually connecting? Studies show that as little as five minutes of real, distraction-free conversation a day with your romantic partner is enough to strengthen your bond. I'm sure the same goes for friendships and family connections. We all have five minutes, especially when the payoff is so large.

In terms of how to limit your exposure to the killjoys, go back to

Week Three on boundaries and get some solid boundaries in place for your own wellbeing.

Places

If you mention the Isle of Arran on the West Coast of Scotland, my heart lights up. I visited it often as a child, as my grandmother lived there. I worked there for a couple of years before and during university, and it's where I met my husband. It's often referred to as Scotland in Miniature because it has all of the elements Scotland is most known for: castles, glorious landscape, the sea, whiskey, art, outdoor activities, great food and more. To say it brings me joy is an understatement.

Where are the places in your life, near or far, that bring you joy? A local park? The architecture of certain buildings near you? A local market that delights your senses? A city or a beach you've visited once? What was it about those places that brings you joy?

Let's get hyper-local here for a second, because we don't all have the time or funds to travel to faraway places. In the place that you live, is there a room or space that brings you joy? For me, I adore my kids' bedrooms. I put a lot of effort into painting them and they feel whimsical. What is about these spaces that I adore? It's the colors, the effort that I put in, the way the light hits them in the morning or at the golden hour. You may not have a lot of living space, but that doesn't mean that the place you lay your head can't bring you joy with some tweaks, like we discussed in the last chapter.

Now, where are the places that suck your joy dry? Standing in line at the grocery store? A heaving crowd waiting for a train? Your cubicle at work? The gas station on the corner where your ex broke up with you?

And what is it about these places that sucks your joy? Does it rub against your values like we discussed in Week Two? I've told you how much I value my time, so long line ups really dampen my joy. Do they serve as reminders for memories you'd rather leave behind? Are the aesthetics sterile or uninspiring?

Now that you know where the most and least joyful places are in your life, how can you increase the former, decrease the latter, or change them in a way that strengthens or weakens their impact? If you work in a cubicle and there's no option to change location, then how can you bring joy to that space? Can you have a little desktop radio, pictures of places you love, or a plant to nurture? And if you have places that bring you joy close to home, can you spend more time in them? I always think it's funny how many houses have beautiful 'front rooms' that go unused. If you like the dining room, why are you only using it for special occasions?

Take stock and make small tweaks. Remember, it is the accumulation of these small shifts that make lasting change.

Things

There is a reason that shows like *Tidying Up* with Marie Kondo and *The Home Edit* are intensely popular – because we want a way to organize and make sense of our things. A key element to the process of both these shows is in editing the things you have, and that's usually based on whether it brings you joy or serves a purpose. Do you actually like and use the things you have?

I'm not saying less is more, but abundance isn't always the answer either. I know that when I KonMari'd my home, I felt lighter, more joyful and was able to see the things that lit me up because they now had more breathing space.

What are the things, the objects, the clothes, the physical items that bring you joy? Why do they bring you joy? Things hold a lot of power. When working with Jen, whose story you heard at the beginning of the book, we found that amidst her busy life, she was able to inject more joy in the simplest of ways – through a teacup. On her honeymoon, she and her husband visited Paris and she bought a vintage teacup. Where had that teacup sat for years? On a shelf. Unused. Isn't that what we often do? We buy nice things and we—say it with me—save it for a special occasion. **Your special occasion is now.** If it brings you joy, start using these items instead of letting them gather dust. Jen started using her teacup each morning for her coffee and each time it brings her a smile and fond memory. What a great way to start your day.

What are the things that kill your joy? A mess of cables that you don't know what they belong to? Stacks of unopened mail that need sorted through? Technology or kitchen gadgets that are half broken and only kinda-sorta work? What about them limits your joy? Lack of use? They're ugly to look at? It was a gift from someone you've fallen out with?

Your things are within your control to do something about. As we know from last week, we crave control, so put it to good use. Can you increase, make use of or give more prominence to the things that light you up? Can you reduce or put out of sight the things that bring you down?

For anyone who has changed clothing sizes and is keeping the old size in their closet – does it bring you joy? Or do you open your closet and it makes you feel some kind of way about your body image? Get rid of it. I'm not saying you have to donate or throw away those clothes, but put the items that don't fit in a box somewhere out of sight. Allow yourself to open your closet and only see things that make you feel confident and most importantly that fit your current body.

Activities

You are in the midst of one activity or another from the moment you wake up until the moment you fall asleep each night. I do not expect one hundred percent of your daily activities to bring you joy, you're not Giselle from *Enchanted* after all. It's also not real life. Adulting is hard. We have real responsibilities from sitting through never-ending meetings to doing our taxes, from commuting to cleaning the cat litter.

It's easy to find the activities that suck our joy. But what activities, large or small, light you up? Is it the walk to the bus stop through a stunning tunnel of trees? Making time to read for a book club during your lunch hour? Catching up with friends? That Zumba class or solo jog? Perhaps it's even a part of your job – not all parts are always fun, but surely there is something (even if it's tiny) that you enjoy doing? What is it about the activity that lights you up? The way it makes you feel, the escapism, the creativity, the freedom or the skill you're developing?

You probably already know what sucks your joy, but make the list anyways while asking yourself why it kills your joy. The why helps you make changes and pivot. When I give corporate workshops, I often have people come up to me afterwards feeling that the only way for them to enjoy work again is for them to quit their jobs. This is almost never the case. Some workplaces are toxic for sure, but in most cases you can pivot how you work, the way you work, your mindset and who you work with in order to make the activity of your work much more joyful. I see it happen again and again.

In our 2021 group cohort of *Stress Less in 90 Days*, each of the participants was going through their own hard situation. While these situations spanned the range of experience, they were each able to increase their joyful activities. Heather began painting again, a passion she hadn't done for years. Fanny made more time in the evening to play with her daughter and began moving her body more regularly. Malena found joy in the simple walks with her dog while she recovered from an injury.

These aren't monumental shifts on the surface, but in practice, when you make more time for things that bring you joy, it adds color and brightness to your day. It's small LEGO blocks that build up over time to give you a solid foundation.

From your list, how can you do more of what lights you up? Doesn't have to be big, just fifteen minutes a day. How can you do less of what drags you down?

Build from there.

Recap

- Notice-Shift-Rewire thoughts and feelings that are holding you back.
- Take an audit of what brings you joy and what dampens your joy.
- Small tweaks in increasing what lights you up and decreasing what drags you down add up to a more vibrant life.
- It doesn't have to cost you a lot of money, time or energy to make these shifts.

WEEK EIGHT
ROUTINES THAT ROCK

As the mother of two young kids, I know that routines can make or break their day. If we decide to be a little more spontaneous and skip nap-time in exchange for a road trip, we know we're playing with fire. It's a gamble we take. Children thrive from routines. Routines let them know what to expect next, what the rules and norms are, how and when to tidy their rooms, when they'll eat, when they play, when they'll sleep. It might sound monotonous, but in fact it helps them to operate at their best. It allows them to stabilize their mood, and let's be honest there is very little that is stable about a toddler. Routines make them feel more secure, and when they feel secure, they are less prone to outbursts and wild tantrums. Take away their routines and tantrums multiply like fruit flies.

Us adults? We may look grown up, but we are giant children who equally thrive off routines. In Week Four we did a deep dive into how to build habits that serve you and break ones that add more stress. In Week Five we learned that so much of self-sabotage comes down to wanting control and defaulting to the easiest behaviors (habits) where we know the outcome, even if it doesn't serve us. We've talked about how to create pockets of joy to elevate your life and boost your energy. This week we're pulling all of that together into routines that will allow you to thrive, sustain energy and stress less.

We've already talked about habits, so what is the difference between a habit and a routine? Well, habits can be intentional (like working out 'x' times a week), or they can be entirely unconscious (which shoe do you put on first?). Routines are a collection of habits that you do again and again, usually in a particular order. How you get to work is a routine. You get up, you get dressed, you deal with any last-minute tasks in the house (pets, kids, what have you), you pick your mode of transport, maybe grab a coffee en route and you're there. Most of these things are done unconsciously (how many times have you driven somewhere and not remembered getting from A to B?), but if we can pinpoint the various routines that you currently have and add some intention so they can begin to help you, you'll be flying.

Why We Need the Right Structure

Has there ever been a time in your life when you felt without structure, or like the structure you had was blown to pieces? Major life changes like a new job, relationship, child, divorce, death of a loved one, moving to a new city, loss of a job, or retirement are common events that shift our routines massively. What's common about them is that these events add or remove an input, whether it be a person, place or thing.

COVID-19 affected us all. Perhaps you suddenly had to work from home, and maybe on top of that you had to add homeschooling some children into the mix. Or maybe you were retired or lived alone so your day to day activities didn't shift much, but it restricted how and when you could see friends and family. Suddenly we were online shopping instead of visiting stores in-person. We had to quickly adapt to the routine of bringing a mask with us wherever we went, washing them and keeping the hand sanitizer or soap stocked.

We all adapted as best we could, given the circumstances.

Humans are adaptable creatures. We created new routines. Now maybe some of them served us—yay to not getting a cold because of increased hygiene—while others made us feel out of alignment. We need some structure in order to not feel like that wind tunnel dude outside a car dealership. We don't want to flail; we want to feel grounded. Structure and routines allow that to happen. Psychological studies show that routines make us feel more calm and in control. Commit to it.

Whether you call it a rule, a standard or a commitment, while it may seem inflexible, what it gives you is mental and emotional space. Mark Manson, the author of *The Subtle Art of Not Giving a F*ck* says "Commitment is freedom, because it hones your attention and focus, directing them toward what is most efficient at making you healthy and happy." Structure and new norms in how you live your life gives you boatloads more than it takes away.

Not all routines are created equal. As we've learned throughout this program, what we value matters. What lights us up and brings us joy and energy matters. If you can build daily, weekly, monthly routines that reflect these vital parts of yourself, they will become easy and they will make you feel whole. You won't have to think too hard about it, because it will become your new normal. You'll crave it.

To figure out where you're going, we need to know where you're at.

Identify Your Current Routines

You already have routines in your life – what are they? Head to the workbook where you'll take note of what routines you currently follow, as well as their impact. For each routine that you can identify, note whether it feels like it adds to your stress, decreases your stress or whether it's net neutral. Only you know how you feel and what the overall impact is on your life.

Some routines don't serve you. They're inefficient, they lack purpose and in the worst case they add stress. It's where that blurred line of habit comes in, because if a routine is not serving you it's likely unconscious. There is zero judgement around them, so be honest about what your go-to routines are. If your routine after dinner is to scroll social media for forty-five minutes or watch back to back episodes of *The Real Housewives*, there is no shame coming from this gal.

If my habit when stressed is to turn to alcohol, this might temporarily give me the ability to numb out, but in the long run I might wake up a little fuzzy each morning. I might even start to build up a baseline chronic anxiety, but never actively deal with it. Or after a long day of work and keeping children alive (the struggle is real), I might zone out in front of the TV. Nothing inherently wrong with that, perhaps it's stress-neutral, but it could mean I now don't have time for other activities that would better allow me to release stress hormones and wind down before bed.

The goal here is not to beat up on yourself for what you are or are not doing. It's to become aware of your patterns, then brainstorm new/altered routines to decrease your tension. Are there new steps in that routine that you can introduce or replace in order to feel better? Or if you're looking at a routine that's actively adding more stress, simply getting to neutral could be a big step for you. It's all about the micro moves.

How to Build a Routine (and Out of What)

If you can build IKEA furniture, you can build a routine. It's one step after another. Often, it's not the "how" to build a routine that people find the most challenging, but what your routine should consist of. If you head to Google, you'll find a million examples of "the perfect routine" for morning, noon and night. We'll talk through some examples this week that could help serve you at home and at work, but none of them will work or last if they don't support your big goal, your values or what makes you tick. Be your own North Star in this process.

I want you to grab a highlighter and go back through the past seven weeks of your workbook. Highlight every action item or behavior shift that has resonated for you. Has going to bed earlier helped you feel more calm in the morning? Highlight it. Has doing the hard thing first each workday made the rest of the day feel easier? Highlight it. Has spending fifteen minutes a week on something that lights you up made you more cheery? Highlight it! Big, small, and in between, whatever those behavior shifts have been that are making you feel more resilient and energetic are, we need to know that full list.

Now that you've got your list of what you've tried and you know works, start to group them by theme. One theme could be time of day; are there some activities that are best for the morning, midday or evening? Another theme could be work life vs. home life.

As you examine these activities by theme, you may start to notice that some of them would quite nicely stack together. For example, you might find that an easily stackable routine is to leave your phone outside the bedroom, have a shower in the evening, moisturize then read a book before bed. Those activities all go nicely together. If that's the case, find the activities that group easily, then determine a time of day or the week that they are best suited for.

In other cases, you simply don't have the ability to stack activities, perhaps because, you know, you work a full-time job! Or as a caregiver your schedule is unpredictable. In situations like these, the routine we're going to build is to take that activity you enjoy/thrive/crave and sandwich it between activities you already do. For example, I know I will log onto my computer at 7:30 to start my work day, and I know I will have a lot of emails waiting for me. Perhaps the new routine is that I sit down at my desk, and before I do anything, I write down a list of my top three priorities for the day, I go to my calendar and earmark time to work on those tasks, and *then* I check email.

It doesn't have to be complicated, but it does need to be intentional.

The Drain of Decision Fatigue

As we discussed in Week Four, we make roughly 35,000 decisions a day, so it's no wonder that our brains are exhausted!

Pre-kids, my husband and I spent three months backpacking Southeast Asia. It was glorious, a trip of a lifetime for sure. I love my husband dearly, but he's not as excited about travel planning as I am. I'd ask him what he wanted to do or where he wanted to visit, and he'd have a couple vague ideas or bucket list items, but the rest was more of a shrug of the shoulders, "Whatever you want to do, babe."

Sounds like a dream, right? And it was at first. I had the mother of all Excel spreadsheets going for this trip. We were visiting four countries, so I researched countless blogs to find out the must-sees, where to eat, the top ten, the top ten that nobody knows about, how to get from Thailand to Laos via a two-day longboat, what currency you need where… you get the drift. I was mega-prepared and excited.

Fast forward to our first night in Laos. Not one of my prouder moments. We arrived after a plane, a train, a tuk tuk and a boat, all in a language and using currencies that we'd never used before. We checked into the hotel I had chosen from a list of twenty. We were exhausted, drained, but then my husband got out his laptop and asked me what I wanted to watch on Netflix.

I'm not going to lie, profanities spewed from my mouth.

When I took a moment to step back and not be so caustic, I realized that I was simply exhausted mentally and emotionally from the toll of making so many decisions in a day. Once I was a little more calm and could articulate that I needed help in planning and booking the rest of the trip, of course my husband stepped up.

That's the thing – we often put off asking for help because we feel like we should be able to do it all ourselves. I hate to burst your bubble, but nobody can do it alone.

Think about how many people have had mini-meltdowns planning a wedding, a birthday party, a trip, a family reunion, hosting a big Thanksgiving dinner or coordinating play dates. God love the event planners of the world, because we mere mortals tend to crack under the pressure of making a million and one decisions.

Making an abundance of decisions is mentally and emotionally exhausting, so our goal is to look at your average week and see how we can minimize decision making so that you redirect energy and clarity toward what is truly important. **Routines can help minimize the number of decisions that we have to make.**

So, let's dive into some examples that you can begin to test out in your own life. Let's look at habits that you can build routines around in the morning, the evening and in the workplace.

Morning and Evening Routines

Don't subscribe to the bullshit that to be successful you need to wake up at 5 a.m. everyday. I know there are a zillion business articles about that, but you know yourself that if you're a night owl, you're a night owl. Regardless of the time your head hits the pillow and comes off it, I encourage you to find a routine to start and end your day so that it's on your terms and nobody else's.

Some examples of habits to incorporate into a morning routine could include:

- Waking up to a body clock alarm instead of the harsh BEEP BEEP BEEP
- Waking up before anyone else in your house for some solo time
- Drinking a glass of water before any other beverage
- Reading a book, journaling or even catching up on your favorite show in peace
- Setting an intention for the day
- Making your bed
- Moving your body, be it a workout or light stretching
- Playing your favorite music or podcast while you get dressed
- Not logging onto social media for an hour

- Being present on your walk to the bus, or listening to an audiobook on your commute

None of these are life-shattering, which is the great thing about them. It's all about the accumulation of micro self-care moments. Maybe you like time to yourself before the day starts, or maybe you prefer to jump out of bed and be go-go-go. Be intuitive about what kind of routine would help you start your day on fire.

In terms of an evening routine, here's what I will say – you need to get good sleep. We've talked about why sleep deprivation is going to add to your stress, so let's make sure your evening routine, be it one step or ten, helps instead of hinders your ability to get a good night sleep.

Some habits that you could build into an evening routine could include:

- A quick journal or brain dump at the end of the work day so you aren't bringing any tension from work home with you
- Cooking a meal
- Dinner with your family, friends or loved ones (without phones)
- Rolling your body on a foam roller to relax your muscles
- A shower or bath with music or a book
- A cup of delicious decaf tea (anything without caffeine or sugar which will make you wired)
- Setting out your clothes for tomorrow, prepping lunches, or any activity that lets you start tomorrow easily
- Time for a hobby you love
- No screen-time for an hour before bed. Perhaps a kinetic activity like drawing, crafting, playing an instrument or doing a puzzle

- Keeping a gratitude journal next to your bed and writing down three things that were great about the day
- Snuggling into bed, putting on an eye-mask and keeping a consistent bedtime

Some of these may resonate, some may be a hell no. Figure out what works for you and what combination. Just remember, your time outside of work is yours. Use it to recharge, for activities and people that light you up, but also to get the rest you need.

Professional Routines That Rock

What does a routine in the workplace look like? Well, let me ask you: what does a normal workday look like? Depending on your job, you might have routine built into it. Perhaps your job has a clear structure where you show up, you do a certain task for a certain amount of time, then the next task and so on and so on.

But for many people, their days are a little more unpredictable. If you're an office worker, chances are your day has a smattering of meetings, and you're constantly juggling e-mails and major projects that you feel like you never complete. I get it. I've worked in customer service! I've also been an event planner. It can feel like so much of your day is out of your control—because it is—and that you're fighting fires.

When you're constantly dealing with micro-emergencies, you're telling other people that they are in fact the priority and that your needs don't matter. You also train them to keep expecting your instant reply the faster you respond. In episode 42 of the Girl Tries Life Podcast, I interview Kyle Toh, the founder of Chic Geek, a non-profit that helps women build thriving careers in technology. I was blown away by how much she accomplished at such a young age. As I was coordinating a date to record the interview, I got an automatic reply from her email that informed me she only checked her email once a day and would respond within the next 48 hours. Talk about a clear boundary. No wonder Kylie had achieved such success not only for herself, but in support of the hundreds of women in tech who have benefitted from Chic Geek. Not only was this a boundary and a habit, but it created a routine for Kylie as to when she would be in a focused state as opposed to response-mode.

What would happen… if the first thirty minutes of your day was dedicated to your deep work? What is deep work? As written in Cal Newport's book titled *Deep Work: Rules for Focused Success in a Distracted World*, deep work is the ability to focus without distraction on a cognitively difficult task. While firing off an answer to that email might feel important (and perhaps it is), is it getting you closer to finishing those projects that propel you forward in your role and your career?

So many of us leave those big projects for the last minute, pretending that we do better in a pressure cooker. In reality, we're not giving ourselves the opportunity to simmer and develop flavor like Julia Child's famed boeuf bourguignon. You probably can't remember the last time you gave yourself the gift of deep work. Experiment with it. Next week, look at your calendar and block out the first thirty minutes to make progress on that project that needs your attention. You may need to set a boundary with your colleagues and communicate what you're doing, but it's worth it. Give yourself a full week to try this out, then come Friday ask yourself if you'd have made this progress without the routine of starting your day with intention.

Here are some other workday habits that you could build into routines:

- Turn off your notifications or pause them during times of deep work
- Set expectations that cameras will be on or off during video calls if you need a break
- Take standing breaks during the day
- Make Fridays (or one day of the week) meeting-free to focus on big projects and catching up
- Make meetings 25 minutes or 50 minutes instead of 30 or 60 so that you have time for bio breaks and/or a mental pause between topics

- Plan your lunches for the week in advance and maybe meal prep a few days at a time
- Plan your outfits for work the night before so it's one less decision
- At the end of each day, write down your top three priorities for the next day so you can start it with intention
- Suggest walking meetings, or take a quick walk during your lunch break. To get out of your head, get away from your desk!

While we're on the topic of work, are you in the habit of hustling? Got an endless to-do list? The idea that more is more, that you have to sacrifice everything in order to succeed? If you are, it's because that's what we've been fed in the media for generations. The tortured artist who only created their best works from times of suffering. The "boss babe" who made it by working around the clock, sacrificing her personal life and never taking no for an answer.

I don't know about you but it sounds freaking exhausting. Don't subscribe to that nonsense.

It is possible to succeed without the habit of burnout. Yes, burnout can be a habit if you live your life by draining the tank and expecting it to be magically replenished in the morning. There are habits and routines that help you stress less and succeed. Asking for help. Doing the hard thing first. Constantly reprioritizing. Learning to let things drop. Scheduling (and actually showing up for) time to take care of yourself. Using your vacation days - and not just to tackle the million and one things on your to-do list. Going to therapy. Working out. Drinking less caffeine. Saying no when you want to say no. Talking to yourself like you would talk to your best friend.

These are all habits, and when we stack them with other activities, they become our routines. Determine which habits make you feel better, stronger, less stressed, and more energetic. Then start building them into your daily life.

Start Small, Ditch 'Should'

Does this mean routines are easy? Not if you try to run before you walk. When you're developing a new habit, start so incredibly small that you for sure can do it. Want to decrease your screen time? Start by five minutes less social scrolling today, then build on that tomorrow. Want to start moving your body more? Stop feeling like a workout isn't worth it unless you do a full forty minutes.

So many people struggle to start a fitness routine because they have a vision of what it 'should' look like. It should be forty minutes. It should be a group fitness class. It should leave me sweaty and tomato-faced. And if it doesn't? So freaking what? Done is better than perfect, and 'done' doesn't have a time stamp on it. Would I prefer to work out without my kids crawling around me? For sure, but if that's not my reality (hello COVID!), then the question becomes "Would I rather have the effect of less stress from consistent movement, or would I rather have one perfect workout once in a blue moon?" I know the answer for me.

Your Identity and Habits

Our identity is who and what we are. Who we are is who we believe we are. To make a habit stick, to make your new routine stick, you need to believe in yourself. Sure, this may all be new to you, so you might worry about whether or not you'll be consistent with it. One of the best tools to have in your back pocket is an 'I am' statement. I am a person who makes my bed every day. I am a person with great boundaries. I am a person who goes to bed on time. You get the drift.

Science supports that we look for evidence to support our beliefs. Whatever your new routine and habits are, write down the 'I am' statement associated with it, put it on a post-it note and leave it somewhere visible. Let this be your anchor for the next few weeks as you build a rock-solid routine.

What happens when the routine goes to shit?

So, you've had a few weeks of really sticking to your new routine. You're feeling good, feeling the benefits of moving more or drinking more water, or spending more time on your hobbies, but then… something throws you off track. Work gets busy. Perhaps your kid goes through a growth spurt and you're not getting the sleep you need. A major life event happens. Suddenly that routine isn't so routine. It's gathering dust, and the idea of starting it up again causes anxiety, guilt or dread.

First, stop being so dang hard on yourself. You're trying something new, of course there will be bumps in the road. Keep hold of an experimentation mindset. Remember I said that you're the best expert of you? This also means you need to discover new ways of being and decide if they resonate or not.

With a new routine that's not gelling, ask yourself why not? Is it that you don't have the right resources, support or time in place? How can you make it inevitable and remove the obstacles in your way? Did you actually ask for help? If not… get on it!

Now let's say you've got everything that you need to do it, but you're still not showing up. Why is that? Instead of judging yourself for not doing it, get curious. When you ask questions, you get answers. Why is it so hard to motivate yourself for this? Does it feel too big? Is there a mindset shift that needs to come first? You may find that by asking these questions you have some a-ha moments, and it's a simple tweak to get started. In other cases, it's the realization that this routine isn't what you need, but what you really need is something else to get to the heart of the matter. Questions will lead you there.

If it is a fit and you've managed to remove the obstacles, just get back up and try. There is a reason my podcast is called Girl *Tries* Life, because trying is the most important piece of life.

I do not expect you to take action on all of the above immediately, but as we discuss routines, habits or new norms you can take to make fewer decisions, figure out which resonate with you the most. Pick the top two or three, write them down in the workbook so you don't forget, and take action on the juiciest one this week.

Recap

- Routines give you freedom, time and energy.
- Habits are often unconscious, whereas routines are a set of intentional behaviors repeated over time.
- Decision fatigue is real – create systems (*cough* routines!) to make fewer decisions and free up brain space.

WEEK NINE

INSIDE-OUT NOURISHMENT

WHAT HAPPENS WHEN YOU REMOVE A STRESSOR LIKE THE TOXIC JOB, that health issue that's been trailing you, or you physically move to a new place to start over? Does the stress just disappear? I'm sorry to tell you that it's just not that simple. Removing significant stressors helps, but I bet you've been in situations where you make the change and you still feel pressure. That's because our lives are complex and stressors compound.

When you focus intensely on one area of your life you can be neglecting another. While your work-life balance has improved, maybe your finances have taken a hit. When you were focused on your physical health, maybe your relationship suffered. So far in this program you've been building some core skills to manage your stress and build a solid framework. Now it's time to look under the hood to see what's been calling for attention that you may not have realized. This week we're going to uncover what the knock-on effect of stress has been on your overall well-being, identify the gaps, and make a clear plan of action to help you feel more balanced and connected.

Burnout is a common stressor many of us face. If you give it your all at work, I bet you are compensating somewhere else. Many corporations rank their employees on an annual basis so they have some standard metric against which they increase your salary. I get why it's done—it makes the math easier—but, suddenly you find your entire worth coming down to a grade. I'm a one or a two or three. If most people are a two, then two is average, right? So you strive for that high point, busting your butt, working overtime, and probably neglecting areas and values in your life along the way.

I did this. I worked so hard to be a 'one'. A one was a high performer. There was prestige. But it led to burnout, frustration and ultimately with me leaving the company. I later talked to former colleagues who had also been high performers and the best description I ever heard was when a colleague told me that to be a one at work, meant she was never a one in any other area of her life. The balance was off.

Redefine Balance

Balance is an elusive term. It implies equality across all areas of your life. Work-life balance makes many feel that there should be an equal division of not just energy, but time. If I work eight hours, and I sleep eight hours, then I should have eight hours to live my dang life. But those eight life hours get quickly and quietly sucked into commuting, making meals, running errands, cleaning our houses. The balance for many of us feels completely off. We give our energy in one place and it's depleted in another.

I want you to try and stop thinking of balance in terms of time. I say that because if you don't stop thinking that way, you're going to be dissatisfied no matter what. In North America, we typically have a 40-hour work week and that's rarely negotiable. If you keep thinking of balance in terms of hours, you'll be frustrated. I can't give my partner, my kids or even myself the same amount of time that I give to my job, so does that mean I'm forever failing the balance game? Not if we redefine it.

Instead, I want you to **start thinking about how each of the buckets of your life make you feel**. How satisfied are you with them, regardless of the amount of time dedicated to them?

One way I enjoy working through this is by using a popular coaching exercise developed by Paul J Meyer called the Wheel of Life. You may have seen a variation of this somewhere but here's the one that I find the most helpful.

These are the eight most impactful categories that can affect your stress. Print off the Wheel of Life page in your workbook at stresslessin90days.ca. You'll really want to have a physical copy. For each category, I want you to shade in how satisfied you are with that area. Start from the center of the circle and shade to the outer edge. The less satisfied you are, the closer to the center your shading is, the more satisfied you are, the farther from the center your shading is, filling in the pie. Do this without judgement or what you *think* the right answer should be.

Let me explain the various categories:

Home

Whether you live in an apartment, a tiny home or on your friend's couch, how satisfied are you with where you lay your head at night? Does it make you feel calm? Would you like it to be tidier? Do you want to be living somewhere else entirely? When you open the door at the end of a workday, how does it make you feel?

Connection

You see people all day long, but do you feel connected to any of them? Connection is that feeling of "they get me, and I get them". Are there people in your life who see you for you, and not what they expect of you? Do you have someone you can call when the chips are down? Do you spend time with anyone who shares your interests and passions? Are you satisfied with your close family relationships? What about romantic relationships? Is that something you want? If you have it, do you feel safe and loved? Overall, how satisfied are you with the connections in your life?

Finances

According to a CNBC article from February 2021[1], 73% of Americans ranked their finances as their number one stressor. How satisfied are you with your current financial state? I'm not talking about where you want to be, but where are you now? How do you feel at this moment? Secure? Struggling? Could be better, but it's okay for now? How does your financial state impact your day-to-day life?

Work

We spend 30% of our lives working and it often feels like more. We move from job to job more frequently than previous generations.

This has a lot of change associated with it, and with change comes stress. Our jobs also lead directly into our financial health, as for the majority of us they are our sole source of income.

Your satisfaction with your work has a significant role to play in your overall stress, but you probably know and experience this already. How satisfied are you with the type of work that you do? How about the specific role and organization that you're at? If you're an entrepreneur, how do you feel things are going? If you're a stay at home parent or a caregiver, this is work too! It's unpaid labor, but it is still work. Are you satisfied with your total compensation (salary, vacation days, benefits) relative to your current role? Your relationship with your coworkers? Your relationship with your employees/supervisor/manager/leader? Is Sunday evening a time of dread for you, neutral or do you look forward to the next workday?

Physical Health

How is your body feeling these days? Energetic? Vibrant? Can you move in the ways that you want to? Do you feel fueled by what you eat and drink? Is anything physically holding you back from the way you want to live your life? Are there niggling issues that you've been meaning to see a healthcare professional about?

Emotional & Mental Health

How is your heart doing these days? Do you feel weighed down or emotionally light? How are you coping with changes that you either opt into or are thrown your way? How do you feel mentally? Foggy? Like a game of Tetris that perfectly came together? How's your self-talk game? Are you getting the emotional and mental rest that you need or are you constantly go-go-go? What content are you consuming and how does it make you feel (I'm looking at you, social media!)? Do you feel like you can regulate your emotions, or is it like driving down a rough stretch of bad road?

Creativity

Have you created anything lately? I'm not only talking about art, but what ideas have you come up with? Have you solved problems? Do you play and try new things? Do you experiment? Do you explore new surroundings, new ideas, talk with people about interesting topics? Do you play or listen to music? Do you build anything? Creativity comes in so many forms, so don't limit yourself in your view of it.

Soul

Whether you call it religion, spirituality, mindfulness or the ability to be in the present moment, soul has a different definition for each of us. The Pixar movie *Soul* explores our meaning and purpose in life beyond what we do, and instead looks at the impact and value of *how* we live and how present we are. Are you content with how you live, how you engage with others and how you show up? This category is a bit nebulous, but I encourage you to really think about what makes your life meaningful, and are you getting enough of that? Or perhaps you're getting enough, but are you present for it? My daughter's laughter lights up my soul, but it's amazing how many giggles I can miss when I'm scrolling Instagram. Are there activities or experiences that help you get into a state of flow, the feeling of being fully immersed and focused?

Does Your Wheel Roll?

Once you've completed your Wheel of Life, right off the bat I want to say, don't panic! Don't be upset if all the categories aren't completely filled out. You will never be at 100% in every area. The pie is never whole. The more important question is would your wheel roll? Is there enough filled out in each category that your wheel would roll either smoothly or even with a few bumps and wobbles? Or are you going to hit a giant pothole and struggle to recover? We can manage bumps, but if you've got a pothole, we need to fill it now.

As you filled in the wheel, were there a ton of thoughts flying through your head? "I could be doing more of this". "I should try that". "I need less of that in my life". There are probably more ideas than you can reasonably take action on right away, so I want you to pick the top two categories that need attention.

The first time I ever did this exercise I was about seven months pregnant with my daughter. Work was a challenge and I was feeling totally off. I didn't know what that 'off' feeling was, but I wasn't myself. I wasn't connected and something was missing. The two categories I selected were physical health and soul. I didn't quite know why I picked soul, but it was calling to me. Physical health, that I totally understood. I struggled with sciatic pain during pregnancy so the heavier that baby got, the more pain I felt walking, sitting, basically any land-based movement. To help with my physical health I tried swimming again. The pain went away in the water. I was able to move and regain energy in an activity that I hadn't tried for years. The surprising benefit, however, was the meditative nature of swimming. You have to regulate your breathing when swimming. It has a soothing rhythm to it. There's the sensation of moving through water, the air hitting your wet skin as your arms come out of the water then dive back in.

This one activity filled two areas of my life that had been calling for attention. It cost next to nothing. I was able to fit it into my weekly schedule, and I began to feel more balanced and whole in my life. Note, I didn't say it was balanced in terms of time, but it *felt* balanced. Was every area of my life perfect? Nope. But this one intentional, focused shift made the world of a difference. I was rolling.

Create a Nourishment Plan

We have our two categories. Within each category, what could you stop, start, or continue doing? What could you take action on in the next seven days? These will be your action items this week - yes, we basically did this week's homework within the chapter itself so that you've got real time for putting them into action.

How will you remove obstacles to ensure that these action items happen? Do you need to set aside dedicated time? Do you need the support of friends, family, or coworkers? Do you need to hit pause on something else so that you create a pocket of time? The laundry can usually wait an extra day...or five.

I want to be really clear that these action items don't have to be huge. For one of my clients, their home life was calling to them. They loved their house and the family dynamic within it, but with two young kids and both her and her partner working full-time, it felt like it was a constant disaster zone. The solution? A collective family ten-minute tidy before they watched TV. That ten minutes meant that when she went to bed at night the surfaces were clear, toys put away, and some of her much needed peace was restored. Naturally the kids would move through the house like a tornado the next day, but she knew that tomorrow night there was a new ten-minute tidy and all would be well. Don't underestimate the difference that the right ten minutes can make to your stress and wellbeing.

And all the other categories? Come back to them. Once you've made traction on these two categories, go to the next ones. Pick action items, work on them, then go to the next category. Do it on your timeline. Take action on the category that calls to you the most, because that's the one that needs nourishment now, not later.

Use the Wheel Whenever You Feel Off

In the future, whenever you're feeling off, or out of balance or like something needs to be fixed, come back to this exercise. It can really highlight a need that may have been missed by your radar. Be honest with yourself when filling it out. Remember that there is no right answer. What matters is how you feel, and helping you feel better bit by bit.

Recap

- Removing a major stressor doesn't necessarily take away the stress.
- Stop thinking of balance in terms of time, instead think about how you feel about each area of your life.
- Would your wheel roll? If not, how can we bolster those areas of life?

WEEK TEN

PERMISSION TO LET IT GO

THE SUMMER I WAS TWENTY YEARS OLD I DID A TWO-MONTH backpacking trip around the world. I met incredible people, ticked off a lot of bucket list adventures, and gained so much confidence and independence. The only downfall of the trip was the weight of my freaking backpack. If you've ever gone backpacking or hiking with a heavy pack, you know what I'm talking about. You have your main backpack with all your clothes, shoes and toiletries, then on your front you carry your day bag. When moving from place to place, I had to be conscious of how I moved, nervous that if I turned too quickly, I could take out an innocent bystander.

I never really trained to carry that much weight, so it definitely came as a shock. I'll never forget getting off my first flight of the trip and being stuck on the London underground in major traffic standing for 40 minutes with both bags. My friend and I finally lugged our way to our accommodation, the straps of our bags cinching at our shoulders. The weight was intense. There was no better feeling than finally dropping our bags and feeling forty pounds lighter.

Smart backpackers learn to streamline. They'll pack fewer clothes, rip sections out of books rather than bring an entire guidebook (this was pre-Kindle y'all), and regularly stock up on travel toiletries rather than carry large quantities. You learn these skills with time and a lot of back pain!

The weight of the stress you're carrying around right now isn't dissimilar. **Stress has an emotional, mental and physical impact**. We talked last week about how you can remove a stressor, but the stress can remain. It's because if we don't learn to let go, we carry a little piece of that stress, grief or trauma with us. Letting go is much easier said than done. This week we'll reflect on all the good reasons we don't let go, and how we can change this.

What Are You Holding On to?

If you've ever been laid off from a job, I bet whenever you apply for a job or have a conflict at work there is a niggling anxiety in the back of your mind - not loudly, maybe, but it's there. If you've ever been cheated on, you're subconsciously on the lookout for red flags. A deep betrayal by a friend, family member or co-worker adds an emotional load and makes you hesitate to open up in future. The impact lingers long after the conflict is 'over'.

What are you holding onto? What frustrations, pain, or trauma are you carrying around with you? What mindset is holding you back? What expectations or limitations are you or others placing on yourself? What are those things that are always niggling in the background?

This is a tough question because it brings up a lot of the things we'd rather leave buried. I want you to know that whatever comes up for you, you're not alone. In doing this work with so many women, I'm continually blown away by the painful experiences people have had and how they've carried on. And yet, often they've carried on while still carrying it with them. You need to drop some of that heaviness.

There are usually two reactions when I say that. The first is, "Yes, I'd love to let go of that, don't you think that's what I've been trying to do? I just don't know how". The second is a reflexive defensiveness. An uncertainty of who they would be, what life would look like, or a disbelief that it's even possible.

This is where I am going to remind you that **if you have trauma that you need to process, please make sure you're getting the professional support that you need and deserve**. We can all benefit from counselling, and there are many programs that can help make counselling more affordable if cost is a barrier. As I said in the beginning, coaching isn't therapy, it's about forward motion and how we can help you achieve your goals. That said, we carry our experiences with us, and they inform the actions we take. You can't separate one from the other.

It's Never "The Thing"

One of the biggest things I've had to process and let go of was the result of my parent's divorce. I was maybe six weeks pregnant with my first child when I found out my Dad had asked my Mom for a divorce. I'm not going to go into the nitty gritty details of why or how, because that's not my story to share, but the impact it had on me was hard and long-lasting. I had this idealistic vision of our family. My parents had been married for thirty plus years, and while they argued and bickered, I still held up their marriage as an example of what I was aiming for, especially as so many friends had divorced parents.

I think when any major revelation like this happens you go back and examine your memories. What was true? What wasn't? I had a rocky relationship with my Dad to begin with, and for a long time I felt really hard done by as a kid. Not that I wasn't provided for - we were definitely financially taken care of - but there were some important moments in my life I felt my Dad was absent for or apathetic about. The divorce amplified these feelings. I was so unbelievably angry. Some of the things I said in the fallout of the divorce were ugly. I don't recognize that version of myself when I think back to that time.

It was in counselling that I realized that what I was carrying was loss and grief. It wasn't the divorce, but the loss of what I thought my family was, and loss of the expectations and hopes that I had. I carried a lot of grief, knowing that my kids would never get to have the same kind of experiences that my oldest niece did with her grandparents. I felt robbed of experiences. I grieved the loss of our family home, never getting that last Christmas with my little baby at the center of attention.

I was also experiencing a lot of uncertainty. The biggest pillar in my life had shifted. If I didn't see it coming, was I that smart or perceptive a person? Did I have poor judgement? If I had poor judgement, what kind of parent was I going to be to my child? During that period, I was an angry, distraught person - would I carry that energy into motherhood?

It. Was. A. Lot.

For many of us, it's rarely the *thing* that is the biggest issue, but rather the ripple effect of the *thing*. It's the culmination of small and large hurts and stressors that go along with the *thing*.

Often, we identify the need to let go, but saying that is so much easier than putting it into action. It's also not one more action item away. There's no magic switch to flip. It's a process. I know, I know, I like quick fixes too, but this is one that truly takes time.

It starts with a decision. Do you want to continue carrying that weight around with you? If you do, that's totally fine. You'll come back to this when you're ready. If not, take a deep breath, and let's begin.

Self-Reflection Exercise

This section is a big self-reflection journal exercise. I'll be asking the same questions that are in the workbook, but providing a little more detail so you know exactly what to look for. Write down the answers as you go in your workbook. **Make sure you're setting aside purposeful time for this.** It's not an exercise to do while commuting or multitasking. Give it the breathing space it needs, probably 30-40 minutes.

. . .

You can download the complete journal questions here stresslessin90days.ca

Begin with a Body Scan

At this point you've identified what is holding you back. When you think of that weight, close your eyes and notice how it feels in your body. Your body can be the first sign of tension before you're even conscious that you're holding onto something and a body scan is pretty much what it sounds like. Take some deep breaths to regulate your heart rate and get the oxygen flowing, then slowly scan up from your toes to the top of your head. Notice every single part of your body from the backs of your knees to the skin on your elbows, your collarbone to the tip of an ear. Take note of every part of your body to see what you're feeling as you think about what is holding you back.

Is there any tension? If so, where? Pay attention to the sensations, discomfort or tightness that the stress is causing you. Yes, I can get a sore back from sitting at my desk for too long, but when I'm stressed because I'm not letting go of a conversation or a frustration, I always feel it in my throat, my shoulders and my lower back. Where do you feel it? This sensation is going to be a marker for you going forward. You'll be able to notice progress not only in how you're feeling mentally and emotionally, but in whether or not your body is holding onto pain.

Why Hold Onto This?

What is the good reason you're holding onto the pain or stressor you've identified? This question is the same question we asked in the self-sabotage chapter. Not letting go of pain, frustration or trauma can be a form of self-sabotage. Remember, self-sabotage is when we are consciously or unconsciously taking steps to inhibit our happiness or future success. We know you need to let go of this weight, but you're obviously holding onto it for good reason. What is that reason?

A common good reason that I hear from clients is a fear of falling apart. *If I actually process what I'm going through, I'll fall apart at work, in front of people I love, or I won't be able to function.* That's a legitimate concern! I would, however, argue that if you don't work on letting it go now, a spectacular falling apart will be inevitable.

Let's start the work now.

Is the good reason one of the reasons we explored in the self-sabotage chapter? Reminder, they are: you fear success, you fear failure, you want control, you want acceptance, you don't feel deserving, you play the blame game and you like the known. The good reason for this can also be protection. You're protecting yourself from the big emotions that will come when you process it. I get it. Whatever that good reason is, write it down. Detail why you think you're hesitant to let go.

The good reason may have nothing to do with self-sabotage, but perhaps it's bringing up other emotions or memories. What are those? Write down the first thing that comes to mind. Don't self-edit or make it sound like you think it "should". This is about being honest. If there's one person in the world you need to be honest with, it's you.

Who Do You Need to Forgive?

Now that you know what is coming up for you and what the good reason is you've been holding onto it for so long, is there something you're holding onto that is tied to another person's involvement? If so, who do you need to forgive in order to let go? Forgiveness doesn't mean what they did was okay. It doesn't absolve their behavior. There's a difference between reconciliation and forgiveness. **Reconciliation is where you want to restore the relationship with whomever it is, and so you need to take certain steps to rebuild trust and/or respect. Forgiveness is about you and what you need. Forgiveness allows you to release anger, frustration and all that focused energy.** It helps you get to your desired outcome. Know that you also don't need to verbalize this to someone - forgiveness is an internal job.

Verbalizing it is a bonus if and only if that makes sense for your situation. More often than not, it's all for you. You don't have to forgive if you don't want to. If you are not there yet, you're not there yet. In most circumstances, time is a big factor in your ability and desire to forgive. Again, if you need the support of a professional, please seek it.

Often, the person we need to forgive is ourselves. Whether you're sorry for not trusting your gut, for your poor behavior, for not being there, or for letting opportunities go by, you did the best you could with your abilities and the information you had at the time. You did. That doesn't mean you don't regret certain things. By forgiving yourself and showing yourself some damn grace, you can move forward. We all make mistakes and falter, but if you're integrating what you learn into how you show up now, that's what matters.

Deep breath. This was a lot.

What Could You Choose to Let In?

Switching gears a little bit, what do you want to make space for in your life? If you weren't carrying that weight, what would you do instead? How would you act? How would you engage with people? Here's some examples I've heard from my clients:

- *If I were able to let go of the pain and embarrassment of being fired, I would apply for a job that I actually liked and ask for the salary I deserve.*
- *If I were able to let go of the resentment of my partner leaving me, I'd start embracing this next phase of my life. I'd do the activities I never felt I could do around him. I'd travel. I'd have adventures. I'd make new friends.*
- *If I were able to let go of the huge expectations I have of my work performance, I'd be able to experiment a bit more and try out projects that I might fail at, but want to explore.*
- *If I were able to let go of needing to know the outcome of everything, I'd be able to be in the moment and trust that it's all*

going to work out. I'd also be able to have stronger relationships where I'm not trying to micromanage everything. I'd be able to freaking relax!

- *If I were able to let go of feeling like I need to work overtime, I'd be able to make space for hobbies I've wanted to try.*
- *If I were able to let go of my parents' expectations of me, I'd be able to fully embrace my sexuality, my identity and my authentic damn self.*

It's powerful stuff, right? Essentially, if we let go of that weight, we know we'll be happier, healthier, more aligned with ourselves. Less stressed. The thing is, you need to help yourself believe that this is possible.

Notice - Shift - Rewire

Fear plays tricks on our brain. It tells us that change isn't safe, and so we retreat and we hold it in. Rewire your brain to focus on the goal. Remember: Notice - Shift - Rewire. Notice the thought that tells you you're a failure, it won't work out, or that you're gonna fall apart. Shift to asking yourself, Is this true? Brené Brown talks about the difference between shame and guilt. "Shame is "I am bad". Guilt is "I did something bad."" So, are you a failure? Or did a certain situation not pan out as anticipated? Are you a bad person, or did you say a bad thing? It's an important distinction.

Now to rewire.

What is a new mindset, belief or perspective that would allow you to flourish? For example, I believe that my business will weather these hard times - I'm playing the long-game, not looking for quick-wins. Or, I believe that I'm worthy of a relationship where my partner respects my boundaries and embraces me exactly as I am. Or, I know I'm a good parent - a few bad moments don't erase my love and care for them.

What is the mindset shift that will serve you in releasing this heaviness?

Add a Touch of Ceremony

To close this all out, similar to the self-sabotage chapter, I'm going to encourage you to hold some sort of ritual or ceremony to let go. Here are some ideas that come to mind:

- Write a letter to the person that hurt you (or to yourself), say exactly what you want to say, then don't send it. Burn it (safely).
- Write a few words that describe what you want to let go on a stone or a stick, then drop it into a running river. Watch it drop to the bottom or float away and visualize the release. If you're planning to do this at the ocean, be conscious of the tide chart so that it doesn't immediately come back to you!
- If and only if your jurisdiction allows it (!), get a sky lantern and either write on it or simply infuse it with intention, light it, then let it go. As it drifts into the sky, breathe deeply.
- Light a candle and think about what you want to release, then slowly blow out the flame. As the smoke dissipates, imagine your tension dissipating as well.

I know those might be a bit woo woo for some, but don't underestimate the benefit of turning a mental struggle into a physical manifestation.

Consistency is Key

Don't expect change to happen overnight. We've brought awareness to what's holding you back and now you have a clear framework to Notice-Shift-Rewire. Use it. Repeatedly. After enough repetition, you will be able to release that weight, take off that backpack and realize how much you were carrying all this time.

As we wrap up this powerful exercise, I want to acknowledge you for the work that you've done this week. This was a big one, but it is so important. I'm not surprised if you're feeling a bit emotionally drained - it's to be expected. I know after an intense counselling session, all I want is to sleep and switch off. It's your body's way of protecting your mind and giving yourself the rest and perspective you need, allowing you to bounce back sooner. Invest in some serious self-care this week.

If you still aren't ready for it now, that's okay. It's here for you to come back to anytime.

Recap

- We carry our past wounds with us. Without intentional steps to release the pain, it will amplify.
- There is usually a good reason you've held onto this pain. Acknowledge and honor that.
- Ceremony or rituals take a psychological wound, make it physical, and allow you to better release it.
- This takes time. Notice-Shift-Rewire on an ongoing basis. Use your anchors as a reminder.

WEEK ELEVEN

THE MOST IMPORTANT RELATIONSHIP

In a world of influencers where we look outside of ourselves for inspiration or motivation, may I remind you that the most influential relationship you'll ever have is with yourself. Nobody can make you do something you don't want to. Nobody can truly make you believe in yourself. You have to walk some of that road for yourself first.

We're at Week Eleven, which means you're about to start on your next 90-day adventure of personal growth. It's critical that you leave this program with supportive self-talk, the ability to rewire for belief in all the amazing things you're capable of, and a strong sense of self-worth. We rarely walk through life alone. We have friends, family, community members who support us, but the most important relationship to cultivate is with yourself. This week we're going to explore all the little ways your brain is going to play tricks on you now and in the future, and how to bounce back with badass resilience.

Negativity Bias

We have a strong tendency to believe the worst in ourselves. It's like when you were an insecure teenager and your parents told you how beautiful/handsome, smart and incredible you were, but you didn't believe it because they were *your parents*. Yet, if you had the opposite growing up, if your caregivers told you that you weren't very smart or attractive or that you were going to fail, you probably did believe them. This is called negativity bias, where you're more likely to believe or remember the negative things than the positive.

If we're wired to believe the negative in what others say about us, that just goes to show how much intentional rewiring we need to do with our own self-talk. I was thinking about this the other day while potty training my daughter. I read one of those three-day potty-training method books, and it put a big emphasis on how to respond to your child when they inevitably pee their pants. What you need to do is not shame them, but to tell them it's going to be okay, that we'll simply try again next time. How about we save a bit of this energy for ourselves? **Next time you make a mistake or embarrass yourself, don't go straight to shame. Give yourself grace.** Tell yourself it's going to be okay and you'll try again next time. Don't you deserve the same kindness you'd extend a child who peed their pants?

Okay, Victoria, easier said than done. If you've got a habit of mentally beating yourself up, this seems like an insurmountable challenge. So break it down. **First, we need to bring some awareness to your self-talk**. What is one of the areas you consistently give yourself a hard time over? The way you look? How you respond (or don't) under pressure? How smart you are?

Our self-talk tends to lump into either worry, all or nothing language, identity statements and our level of self-confidence.

Worry Less, Live More

If you consider yourself an overthinker or a worrier, you're not alone. I can't pull a current statistic for this one, because I feel like

COVID-19 ratcheted it up ten million percent, but pre-pandemic in the U.K. roughly 86% of people self-identified as worriers. Worry, stress, anxiety and depression have taken a sharp uptick over the last decade, and many are suggesting a pretty strong correlation to smartphones entering our lives.

You now have the ability to be connected and 'on' 24/7. While your life wasn't without stress a decade or more ago, you certainly weren't experiencing the same runaway train of content barreling into your brain. Each fresh news article or social media post is a marker for you to compare yourself against, something to think about, be concerned about, etc.

My worrying went through the roof once I had kids. When I met my husband, he had a motorbike, and it's long been a discussion since he moved to Canada that he'd like to get a bike again. I rode on the back of that bike a few times in Scotland and it was a lot of fun. Adrenaline surging fun. But now, while I'm not so concerned about him riding that bike, the idea of both of us being on it together freaks me out. My brain goes to catastrophic thinking, and what if we were in an accident and both of us were injured or died. I go dark.

According to clinical psychologists, **roughly 85% of the things that we worry about, never happen**[1]**.** Not only does it not happen, but it usually has either a positive or a neutral outcome. Hurray! So, if we logically know this, why do we still worry, and how the heck do we calm it down?

The first step is to **ask yourself is this true**? Will I die on the back of that motorbike? Odds are unlikely. I have higher odds of making it to my 100th birthday[2] than I do of dying on the back of a motorbike. That's actually quite uplifting.

Next, ask yourself **can you solve this problem that you're worrying about**? I have a simple choice in this example - I can choose not to get on that bike. If it makes me feel better, and I don't feel like I'm losing out, then this is definitely solvable.

What about if you're diagnosed with a terminal disease? Odds are not solvable, right? So, in a case like this you have choices to make. With the information you have available, how are you going to continue to show up with whatever time you have left? Obviously, emotions will run high and low and everything in between, but **you have choices**.

Randy Pausch was a professor of computer science at Carnegie Mellon University who was diagnosed with terminal pancreatic cancer in 2006. He was told he had no more than six months left to live, and this was a forty-six-year-old man at the time who had three young kids. It's devastating and it's not fair, but how he chose to live out the remainder of his life was nothing short of incredible. I encourage you to take a pause, go to YouTube and search for "The Last Lecture" by Randy Pausch. It is one of the most inspirational speeches I've ever seen. It was a love letter to his kids, his community, his family and everyone who shaped him. It was also a choice to leave a legacy amidst a terminal diagnosis.

Finally, I want you to **ground yourself**. Just like last week, when you're feeling the worry take over, pause and engage in a body scan meditation. Take some deep belly breaths, get that oxygen deep into your stomach, exhale and repeat. As you regulate your breathing, start from your toes and move to your head. Notice all the sensations throughout your body one by one. How often do you stop and think about how your elbows or your kneecaps are feeling? Take a minute, do it.

Grounding yourself in the present moment as often as you can will help you stay out of future-state worry-mode and stay in the current reality. Because what you're worrying about, as we have seen already, is statistically fictional. Be here. Feel your feet on the earth, and focus on what you can do right now.

All or Nothing

I'm willing to bet you've said things like *I'm never going to get that job*, or *I always screw up*, or *I'm always single*, or *I never follow through*. Or you use this language with the people in your life. *He always leaves the toilet seat up. My coworker is always annoying. My kids never listen to me. People never recognize how hard I work.*

Can you say with certainty that one hundred percent of the time these statements are true? My kids sometimes listen to me, my husband sometimes remembers to put the toilet seat down, and I sometimes do follow through depending on if it's important enough to me. You see? Unless you have empirical data to back that statement up, **what all or nothing language does is close off your mind to other possibilities**. In psychology this is the difference between a fixed mindset (this is the way it is), as opposed to a growth mindset (this is what it could be).

One of the quickest ways to start pulling back on this language is to self-edit in the moment. As soon as you hear the word 'always' or 'never' come out of your mouth, check yourself and ask if that's true. If it's not, then change the language in real-time.

Let's go one step further and say it doesn't even matter if the word comes out of your mouth. When you are thinking always or never thoughts, bring up a giant stop sign in your mind and rephrase it. You do you, but particularly with self-talk, one of the strategies I use is to snap (lightly) the hair elastic that lives on my wrist as an extra reinforcement. Anything physical (like an anchor) can help snap you out of a nebulous thought (pun intended). Please don't go about injuring yourself, but maybe clap your hands together, take a deep breath, shrug your shoulders up and down, press your feet into the ground, or shake your head. Some form of physical action can help both bring awareness to the self-talk habit you want to break, and the rewiring you're doing by rephrasing the language.

Identity Statements

How you talk about yourself goes beyond all or nothing. It's also about who you say you are, or aren't. I'm an overachiever, I'm a quitter, I'm *just* a [insert role here], I'm not loveable, etc. On the flip side, are there pieces of yourself that you rarely talk about? Are you afraid of what people will think? Will they laugh or tell you you're not good enough?

For the longest time I struggled with saying that I am a Stress Reduction Coach. Given my history of being a stress-ball, I worried

I'd be judged for it, or that people would roll their eyes. Now I think, so frigging what? Having bad days doesn't take away from who I am or the skills I've learned. Nor does a bad day take away your identity.

So, who the heck are you? Who do you know that you are deep down, even if it hasn't come to fruition yet? You know the importance of identity statements when it comes to habits and routines, as we discussed in Week Eight. If you start talking in the present tense, for example "I am a damn good mom", then your brain starts to look for evidence that this is true and opportunities to reinforce the behavior. Call it manifesting or a self-fulfilling prophecy, but 'I am' statements are powerful.

Instead of thinking that the perfect version of yourself is ninety days or a year or a decade from now, if you identify right now as a loving parent, thoughtful friend, hard worker, or a person with rock-solid boundaries, you show up differently, and probably in ways that you desire. But you need some repetition of this.

Make sure you are rewiring the self-talk that tells you you're not enough or it's out of reach, and start telling yourself that you are enough and that you're building your dream now.

Before you go and figure out how you want to identify, ask yourself if it's on your terms or someone else's. Nowadays I need to be super clear with myself of my worth, both at home and at work, so that I don't run the risk of letting someone else's appraisal of my identity ruin my day. Someone else might consider me average, but I now have enough sense of self and my worth that I know whether or not I'm killing it. I just won't kill myself to meet their definition. On Instagram @thefemaleconquerors said "I don't care who is doing better than me. I am doing better than I was last year. It's me vs. me." Take this energy into how you talk to yourself and how you identify with your goals.

An exercise that can be helpful for this is to pick the statement you want to reinforce, then get in front of a mirror and repeat it to yourself again and again and again until you start to feel it. Warning - other emotions may start to bubble up and that's okay!

Look yourself in the face and tell yourself you're worthy, because you are.

Confidence

Stress and confidence are opposite ends of the spectrum. If you're high in stress, you're low in confidence. If you're low in stress, you're higher in confidence. In many cases, low confidence comes from the stress of uncertainty. We can know one thing for sure, but be uncertain about the outcome in another area. For example, you could have the utmost faith in your skills in the workplace and be confident about how you are as an individual performer, but still be stressed about your annual performance review because you lack confidence in the people who are assessing you and how you are being perceived.

To me, there are three key components to building and strengthening your confidence. It's a little acronym I like to call **ACE: Alignment, Consistency and Evidence.**

Alignment

Your values are your north star. If you are behaving in a way or are put in a situation that is counter to your values, your confidence will wane. It won't feel right, you'll doubt it. It's not to say that things can't still work out — anything is possible — but whether or not you *feel* confident will be affected. Whether you're struggling with your confidence about your work, a relationship, your performance, your creativity, etc., go back to your values from Week One and see if you're in alignment or not. If you're not, what do you need to do to bring yourself back to center?

Consistency

There are very few people who do something once and then have the innate confidence that they are an expert forever. Those that do feel that confidence are probably narcissists. A certain orange-haired man comes to mind.

If your performance, your interactions or your behavior is as unpredictable as which line at Costco will end up being the fastest, then it's hard to feel confident. You're all over the place. You can't predict where you'll go. You're inconsistent.

Consistency is key. What habits can you begin forming to show up more consistently, to continually act in alignment with your values? Or if it's learning a new skill or starting a new job or a relationship, there's a certain amount of repetition and practice that needs to be in place to trust in yourself, others and organizations. If you want to become more confident, first become more consistent.

Evidence

There will always be naysayers. In the words of Taylor Swift, "Haters gonna hate, hate, hate, hate, hate." If every author believed their worst review, they'd never write another book. The challenge with evidence is that it's hard to pull on when you're feeling low on confidence. You'll look for every example that you're wrong – remember negativity bias? I need you to build up that evidence now.

Hannah Cree, a mentor who I deeply admire and have had on my podcast twice[3], once shared her struggles with imposter syndrome. **Imposter syndrome is when you perhaps doubt your efforts, or believe your successes aren't deserved.** It's the nosey neighbor of low confidence.

Hannah suggested that I keep a physical or digital file of all the evidence of my success. Every great testimonial - pop it in there. Every positive review, kind word, achievement of success, mark it down. We know that negative information likes to take center stage in our mind, but this file of evidence is something tangible you can return to when your confidence needs a boost. I've done this and I can't stress how valuable an exercise it is. So go do that! It doesn't have to be tied to your work, but perhaps it's evidence of how good a parent you are, what a valuable friend, how thoughtful a partner, what a good doggie parent, community volunteer, etc. Pull that evidence together and review it frequently.

With the ACE elements, confidence will grow over time. No doubt about it.

Change Is the Constant

If you're watching a movie or a TV series and the main character is the same at the end as they were at the beginning, it's rarely satisfying. We like to see growth, an arc of transformation. Ironically when we're going through that growth, we rebel against it. We let all the voices of the outside world and our monkey mind dictate who's in charge. I'm here to tell you that you are in charge, if you choose to be.

Nurture this relationship with yourself. As with any relationship, you might bicker with yourself or give yourself the cold shoulder from time to time, but make sure that more often than not you're showing up to give yourself the care, support, and loving words that you need to thrive.

Recap

- Don't neglect your relationship with yourself - it's the most important one you'll ever have.
- What we worry about rarely comes to be, so instead ground yourself in reality.
- Remove all or nothing language from your vocabulary.
- Place goals and identity statements in the present tense.
- Confidence is ACE: Alignment, Consistency and Evidence.

WEEK TWELVE

WHAT COMES NEXT?

In the words of *The Good Place*, "Holy forking shirt balls!" You're here. You made it. It's Week Twelve and you haven't put this program down, even though it's been a challenge. Change always is. Maybe you took some breaks and came back to it. That's okay! You came back to it. I'm so freaking proud of you.

I have a lot of feels when it comes to Week Twelve, partly because I hate saying goodbye to people. Writing this chapter feels so bizarre and odd, because usually in group coaching or one-to-one coaching, I get to celebrate directly with you the progress that you've made. I get to share the change that I've seen in you, the change you may not have noticed for yourself, and I get to hear in your own words what's changed for you. It's such a powerful moment for both of us. Writing a book is a one-way deal. I've shared this structure with you to manage your stress, but I haven't necessarily been there to cheer you on along the way. This is a moment where I'm selfishly going to ask you to reach out. Message me on Instagram, contact me through my website, whichever works for you. I would be so honored to hear how this program worked for you and what changed. I would love to share in this moment with you.

What Comes Next?

Okay, gushy feelings aside, I think the end of any program comes with highs and lows. You've had a clear structure to work from for ninety days, so there can be a real uncertainty around what comes next. I don't for a second want to leave you hanging. Week Twelve is where we look back and create a clear plan for going forward.

I'm going to guide you through some journal questions in this chapter that you'll also find in the workbook at stresslessin90days.ca. Grab a cup of tea, create a calm space for this in your day and let's do this.

Your Personal Highlight Reel

Remember in Week Zero where I said in real life we don't get that Rocky training montage highlight reel moment? Well… it turns out, you do. Each week in the workbook you've recorded your Wins This Week (WTWs), large and small. Right this second, I want you to pause reading this and go back and read your WTWs back to back.

I'm sure sometimes those wins didn't seem like much in the moment, but when you string them together, when you suddenly see how much progress you've made and the beautiful moments you've had in ninety days, suddenly it feels much more impactful. The beauty of this is you can keep going. You can keep tracking your weekly wins. Grab yourself a little journal or notebook and keep this practice going. Whenever you need a reminder of how far you've come as you navigate this journey to less stress and personal growth, your collection of WTWs can be that highlight reel.

Looking Back to Look Forward

Highlight reel in mind, now I want you to think back over where you were ninety days ago, and where you are now. What were those shifts and changes? Large or small, I want you to write it ALL down. It all matters. I often find it's the small, possibly imperceptible shifts that are most meaningful to your growth. It's an inside job, so don't underestimate the impact of a new attitude, belief, habit or routine. What do you do now that you didn't before? What do you believe now? How has your thinking changed? Write it all down. Don't worry about the bumps in the road, we'll get there soon. Start with what went well.

As you look back over what you've written, I want you to vocalize the progress you've made. *I did this. I showed up. I took charge of my own life.* Say it out loud. Write it down. Your brain needs evidence to cement this. We so easily acknowledge the progress that others make, while we downplay our own efforts and progress. Not today. Today you honor you. Because you are mother-trucking worth it.

So, what if you're sitting here and you're thinking to yourself that perhaps you didn't make quite the change that you wanted to. What then? Honestly, very rarely do people end up exactly where they expected to be after ninety days. Sometimes goals shift as we evolve our thinking, our values change, or we are thrown an unexpected, uncontrollable hiccup. I've had clients who have begun *Stress Less in 90 Days* a week after being asked for a divorce, or their parents were hospitalized mid-program, or COVID-19 struck. **Rarely are we gifted the perfect set of circumstances in which to do this work.** Unfortunately, that's life, but the fact that you're reading this chapter and you're still here means **you showed up. You kept going.** There is nothing more impressive to me than when people show up even in hard times. Recognize that.

There are other reasons we may not achieve our goals. Sometimes we set the expectations far too high. We don't know what's possible or realistic. Bill Gates said, "Most people overestimate what they can do in a year, and underestimate what they can do in ten years." Ninety days is often the same, but recognize how much further ahead you are than you'd have been if you didn't start. Now you can use this insight going forward when you set new goals. This is also why I encouraged you in Week One to outline how you wanted to feel. You might not have quite achieved a clearly outlined goal, but perhaps you are feeling the way you wanted to feel. That is much more important. Targets and metrics can always be hit eventually. Feelings matter now. **You live in your body, heart and mind every single day, so how you feel matters**.

As we said in Week One, when you are accountable to the right people, you are up to 95% more likely to achieve your goals[1]. Did you find someone to be accountable to? Did you check in with them weekly and share the highs and lows? Or did you let that go a little bit? Were they the right person? Did they give you that support, but also the tough love when you needed it? The right person or people can be hard to find. It's entirely possible that you self-sabotaged from the get go. As we learned in Week Five, when we fear failure or success, we often stay quiet and don't reach out for help. Was that you? That's okay. Or maybe it felt too hard to tell someone that you were doing a program like this. I get it, I hear it from people all the time. There is a stigma around saying that you're stressed or burnt out. You don't have to tell everyone, but find the right person as you look to the next ninety days.

This is where I see the power in group or one-to-one coaching. They both offer different benefits, and suit different personality types. In the 2021 cohort of *Stress Less in 90 Days* we tried something different. We veered away from a Facebook group where they could share their action items and their WTWs, and instead created a WhatsApp group. I was blown away by the impact of this. I'm writing this chapter five months after the conclusion of the official program, and those ladies are still connecting weekly with one another. They came into the program strangers from across North America, with different needs and goals, and they left as each other's cheerleaders. They're so open and vulnerable with one another about when hard days happen, because they will. During the program itself, we were able to call on one another's skill sets. Little did I know that every member of that cohort was in a job that had billable hours. I've never had to process that, so they could provide support and guidance for one another in a way that myself or my co-creator couldn't. This is the power of group coaching - it's the power of the many.

For others, one-to-one coaching fits their needs and their lifestyle better. They want to dive deep and focus solely on their challenges for the week ahead and I help them do that. I remind them of the goals they set, I ask the tough questions, and I cheer them on as they go through the messy middle, as my friend Steph calls it.

Whether it's working with a coach or not, **finding the right people to be accountable to statistically changes the outcome**. It reminds me of when I would try to go jogging on my own. I would start, stop, start, stop. Staying motivated on my own, with just my headphones was a challenge. But when I signed up for a 10k, suddenly I had a clear goal, I was accountable to the folks that had donated to the cause I was supporting, and on race-day itself I ran with the fewest breaks I'd ever taken because of that community of runners moving together. I would be spurred on by the folks on the sidelines with their funny posters and their cowbells. Maybe you've experienced something a little bit like this before? Did you have it in place for this program? If not, make sure to find it going forward.

Your Go-To Tools

I said at the beginning of the program that you know yourself best, but that there's still a lot to discover. Trying this program was a new structure for you, maybe something you've never done before, exercises you've never tried or ideas you'd never considered. I have no doubts that it didn't all gel for you. What works for one person, doesn't always work for the next. So, now, let's do some assessment and investigation so you can take the right tools forward.

Put aside the actual change that happened right now, when you think back on the tools that I gave you, the action items, the strategies to try, which of them resonated the most for you? What is a tool you're one hundred percent keeping in your toolkit going forward? Which ones will be reserved for specific moments (I'm thinking self-sabotage in particular here)? What a-ha moments or realizations about yourself did you have?

And then what didn't work for you? Did something feel too woo woo? Did it rub up against your values? For some reason my mind is filling up with that TikTok video of Tika the dog in all the outfits. "Love it, couldn't wear it!" Which strategies were "Tried it, didn't like it"? In my years of counselling, coaching and being coached, there are many strategies I've experimented with and they just weren't right for me; others swear by them. Knowing what doesn't work for you is just as powerful as knowing what does. Curate that list, then edit going forward.

The last question I want you to ask yourself is what did you learn about yourself? Did you learn that you're capable of more? Or that you really were carrying something that needed to be released? That your feelings are valid? What realization did you have about yourself as a human being?

Your Next Ninety Days

This assessment of what works, doesn't work, a-ha moments and self-realizations is your foundation for moving forward. From here, I'm going to suggest you set a new ninety-day goal. Repeat the same process from Week One. Where do you want to be in ninety days, realistically with a stretch goal? How do you want to feel? What support and accountability do you need in place to make this happen? When are you going to start? Maybe that goal is to continue with fiery purpose. Maybe the goal is rest and relaxation. Your goals and needs are yours and yours alone.

Ninety days is a season. It's a relatively short but impactful period where you can focus on a goal and make significant progress. And you've done it, you've proven that you can do it once and you can do it again. If we're lucky enough to live to the age of eighty, that's 324 ninety-day cycles. Think of all that you've done in the past ninety days, and all that you're capable of doing going forward. So often we think there's not enough time to do or achieve the things we want in life. There is enough time! There's enough time if you're intentional, while also honoring your mental, emotional and physical needs in the process. Hustle culture makes us feel it all has to happen now. Let this past ninety days be the proof to you that you can make change in your life AND manage your stress and wellbeing. Two things can exist at the same time, if we choose to reject the go-go-go mentality and instead embrace being and growing.

You can always come back to this ninety-day structure. When things start to get tough or just too much and you know something needs to change, start your own ninety days again. The activities and learnings from each week are evergreen. They'll mean something different to you at different stages of your life. Let this be a safety net of structure that you can hold onto when needed. I do. All the time.

Letter to Your Future Self

When I started Stress Less Ladies, I participated in a small business accelerator that was not unlike group coaching. Each week we learned new content, reflected, set action items, and the cohort of small businesses cheering one another on was incredible accountability.

One of the last exercises that they had us do was to write a letter to our future self, a letter that we'd receive in the mail in six months. I want you to do a variation of this now. Obviously, I can't send you your letter, but once you write it, I want you to put it in a safe place, then set a calendar reminder for six months from now. Perhaps in that calendar notice you also write down where you left the letter - am I the only one that loses things all the time?

When writing this letter, think about where you want to be in six months. What changes do you hope to see? The first part of the letter should be along the lines, "I hope that…" and insert your goals and wishes. Talk about the change that you hope you've achieved.

The second part of the letter is where you write the words you'd want to read if you haven't achieved those goals. How are you going to build yourself back up? What grace can you offer your future self? What words of motivation will you tell yourself to get going again? How can you acknowledge that the future you is a badass no matter what? Don't forget this, it's critical.

You can add anything else into this letter that you want (maybe throw $20 in there - I always like finding random cash in the future!), seal it up, put it somewhere safe and forget about it. You will. Then when that notification goes off in your calendar it will be an awesome surprise. I adore hearing from clients when they get their letters in the mail after our group or one-to-one coaching together.

Celebrate This Moment

You've acknowledged how far you've come, so now have a friggin celebration! Whatever that means to you. A glass of champs, a dinner with friends, a day off, a dance party, whatever it is do something special to mark the completion of these ninety days. It was a huge project, but you did it. It's important to mark the milestones. I hope you do something special for yourself, and I selfishly hope that you send me a note or tag me on social to tell me what you did. I want to cheer you on as well!

Goodbye for Now

Remember I said I hate goodbyes? I'm viscerally feeling this in my body right now. I haven't even met you in person, but I just know that if you got this far in the program, you're special. You showed up for yourself and you were on a mission to stress less. So, while I don't *know* you, I know you. And I know you're awesome. It's hard saying goodbye to awesome people, so let's not say goodbye forever, but goodbye for now.

You've got this.

Cheers to the next ninety days.

ACKNOWLEDGMENTS

This book has been a labor of love. I'd like to say that it was written on a glorious Italian retreat in the countryside, not a care in the world, watching the sunset as I typed away on my computer, but it wasn't. It was written during a devastating and exhausting global pandemic in tiny pockets of time, with help from so many people. People who shaped it, people who provided their feedback, and people who cheered me on when I had my doubts.

First and foremost, to my husband, David, and our kids, Jack and Anna. Thanks for giving me the time and space that I needed. David, thank you for taking on a much larger parenting role so I could make this dream a reality. Jack and Anna, I'm hoping I wasn't too absent(!), but thank you for your patience with Mummy as she juggled all the roles.

To my brother, Neil, thank you for being a sounding board, but mainly for being an incredible editor. From where this book started to where it is now, the transformation is in large part down to your astute edits and feedback.

To my Mum, Diana, thanks for always believing in me and reminding me that I'm capable of hard things. I have so appreciated all the babysitting, and big thank you for the weekend at your place when I powered through 20,000 words! My fingers still cramp at the memory.

To my sister-in-law, Tara, thank you for your early feedback and editing. The simple phrase of "This is a book I'd buy," from a reviewer of your caliber has carried me through a lot of moments where I lacked motivation and inspiration.

To my Dad, thank you for your support as we moved West.

To Amy Stubbs, for your many years of wise counsel and for being one heck of a coaching partner.

To Hannah, for the call that I needed the most at the time I needed it most.

To Families Matter and in particular to my postpartum counsellor, Amanda, for getting me through rock bottom. I am eternally grateful for the services you provide.

To my cover designer, Sheena, thank you for creating a cover I'm so proud of.

To Lorraine Paton, thank you for getting me through the process of publishing and keeping this scatter-brain on track.

To all the people who support my life and my business in so many ways, thank you. Special thanks to Stephanie Pollock, the best business coach an entrepreneur could ask for, and Amy Wood, my phenomenal PR manager.

To my coaching clients, past and present, you are the reason I do this work. I am honored by the vulnerability you've shared with me, impressed at your resilience and the way you show up even when times are tough. To the clients who have allowed me to share your stories in these pages, an extra special thank you.

RECOMMENDED RESOURCES

Stress Less in 90 Days

- Group Coaching. New cohorts start every January, registration by end of December.
- One-to-one coaching with Victoria. Limited spots available each quarter. Email victoria@stresslessladies.com to enquire.

Reading

- The Joy of Being Selfish by Michelle Elman
- Atomic Habits by James Clear
- Intuitive Eating by Evelyn Tribole and Elyse Resch
- High Performance Habits by Brendon Burchard

Watch

- The Last Lecture by Randy Pausch

Listen

- The Girl Tries Life Podcast (many of the women featured in this book have joined the podcast as guests)
- Unlocking Us with Brené Brown Podcast

ABOUT THE AUTHOR

After contracting shingles twice before the age of thirty, Victoria Smith knew she had to recalibrate her relationship to stress. Following her own wellness journey, Victoria became certified as a health and a life coach, focusing on stress management. As the founder of Stress Less Ladies Ltd, Victoria helps women to significantly reduce their stress so that they can thrive personally and professionally. She does this through corporate speaking, individual and group coaching, online programs, the Girl Tries Life podcast, and this book. Victoria Smith is a speaker, stress reduction coach, podcast host, entrepreneur and author.

For more information on coaching or speaking opportunities, please contact victoria@stresslessladies.com

facebook.com/stresslessladies
instagram.com/stresslessladies
linkedin.com/in/victoria-smith-stressless
pinterest.com/stresslessliving
goodreads.com/stressless

NOTES

Week Zero

1. https://www.apa.org/monitor/2011/12/exercise

Week Six

1. https://open.spotify.com/episode/6C0SWubMMHFtbtSbrKLkcY?si=NvOGmeHzS32JqZggjZkTqw

Week Seven

1. Jessica's Girl Tries Life interview - https://www.girltrieslife.com/podcast-153/
2. Linda's Interview https://www.girltrieslife.com/podcast-146/
3. https://linda-hoang.com/category/unexplained-infertility/
4. https://www.girltrieslife.com/podcast-142/

Week Nine

1. https://www.cnbc.com/select/73-percent-of-americans-rank-finances-as-the-number-one-stress-in-life/

Week Eleven

1. https://www.nbcnews.com/better/pop-culture/praise-worry-why-fretting-can-be-good-you-ncna757016
2. https://stacker.com/stories/2343/what-are-chances
3. https://girltrieslife.podbean.com/e/common-good-radio-love-and-problem-solving-with-hannah-cree/

Week Twelve

1. https://observer.com/2017/03/psychological-secrets-hack-better-life-habits-psychology-productivity

Made in the USA
Middletown, DE
23 October 2021

50745002R00106